A History of
CAMP OWATONNA
1922-2021

A History of
CAMP OWATONNA
1922-2021

J. R. SUBER

Copyright © 2021 by Camps Newfound and Owatonna.

All rights reserved. No part of this book may be reproduced or used in any manner without written permission of the copyright owner except for the use of quotations in a book review.

This is a work of nonfiction. The events in this work have been set down to the best of the author's ability. Every effort has been made to trace or contact all copyright holders. The author will be pleased to make good any omissions or rectify any mistakes brought to his attention at the earliest opportunity.

The images in this work have been used with permission. They are from various collections, including Camps Newfound and Owatonna, as well as Phoebe (Pemy) MacKenzie Smith, the Treworgy family, Glenn Johnson, Jamie Bollinger, Scott Moeller, Rich Coomber, Carol Ryan Hilton. Several photos from the 1980s come from photo albums that were given to Camp by Helen Eddy, the mother of Selby Eddy, a beloved camper and counselor in the 1980s and early 1990s.

For inquiries, contact:

Camps Newfound and Owatonna
4 Camp Newfound Road
Harrison, ME 04040

Version 20210817

To Spencer, Collin, Mike, and Emac, my cabinmates and my mentors. And in honor of Garrett.

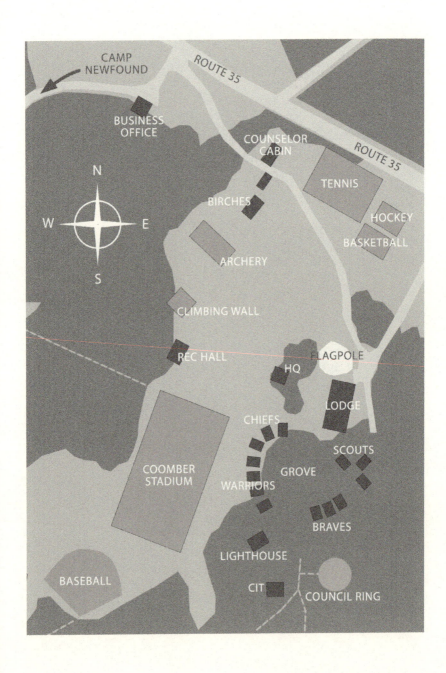

Table of Contents

Foreword ix
Author's Note xi

Part I: Camp Ropioa
George A. Stanley, Founder of Ropioa 1
The Stanley Years (1922-34) 8
The Lowe Years (1935-40) 33
Interim Years (1941-55) 39

Part II: Camp Owatonna
1950s
Founding Camp Owatonna (1955) 47
First Summer with Tom Hilton (1956) 55
The Edwards Years (1957-63) 67
1960s
The Anderson Years (1964-66) 89
The Beyer & Ullom Years (1967-68) 99
1970s
The Bower Years (1969-75) 107
The Schulze & Cole Years (1976-80) 117
1980s
The Cady Years (1981-84) 125
The Clark, Crandell, & Martin Years (1985-89) 129

1990s
　The Johnson, Taylor, & Bollinger Years................. 139

2000s
　The Martin, Brantingham, & Frank Years.............. 153

2010s
　The Bless, Pelton, & Charlston Years..................... 169

Appendix

　Directors... 181

　White Feathers.. 182

　Black Feathers... 184

　Greens Plaques.. 186

　Blues Plaques.. 188

　Reds Plaques... 190

　Golds Plaques.. 192

　Miscellaneous.. 194

　Acknowledgements... 201

　Endnotes... 203

　Index.. 228

　About the Author.. 232

Foreword

We are celebrating and honoring the 100th anniversary of the founding of Camp Ropioa and Camp Owatonna with a reunion at Camp from September 3-6, 2021. As part of that celebration, we felt it was important to tell the history of those 100 years, which has led to the writing of this book. Camp Owatonna, born out of Camp Ropioa, has a unique and storied history. As I think about it, I'm in awe of the vision that several Ropioa alumni had when they established Owatonna as a non-profit Christian Science camp in 1955, essentially reactivating Ropioa after it had been run as a non-denominational camp for the 15 years prior. The story of our beloved camp's journey back to being a Christian Science organization is told in great detail in this book.

Peoples' love for Owatonna today is born out of the traditions and legacy that have been maintained for a century. Those that have had the great opportunity to attend or work at Owatonna and Ropioa know the impact these camps have had on them, wherever their journey has taken them. Camp encourages everyone to develop their deepest character and best self at a place where friendship, love, and spiritual growth are paramount. Camp's long-term success has lied in always going back to its origin and higher mission to serve young people in a thriving Christian Science community.

The same vision and mission that began with Ropioa in 1922 and continued with Owatonna in 1955 is still very much alive now. Today, our vision statement reads: "Our vision is for campers and staff to learn and demonstrate complete trust in God in a unique Christian Science community"; and our mission is to "serve campers in a place where Christian Science is lived and loved, through overcoming limitations, nurturing spiritual growth, promoting spiritual discovery and having fun."

We can't be grateful enough to those who have committed themselves to keep the vision of Camp alive over many, many years—Trustees, Directors, staff members, families, campers, foundations, and donors. And none of it would be possible without the campers and staff who come each summer from across the United States and a few foreign countries to all join together to create and live in a great residential camp experience.

My family has certainly benefited a great deal from its connection with Camp as campers, counselors, and Directors, going back to the late 1950s. We hope you'll stay connected to Camp. We love hearing from you near and far about where your life's journey has taken you. It can't happen without you and your love of Camp, and we hope you'll enjoy this history of Ropioa and Owatonna.

With love and appreciation,

Seth "Chic" Johnson
Executive Director
Camps Newfound and Owatonna

Author's Note

One hundred years ago, our Camp was established to be a home away from home for Christian Science boys. It is impossible to document all the immeasurable good that has been lived here in the century since. Countless moments of brotherhood, growth, laughter, and healing—these are etched more meaningfully and vividly within each of us than could ever be recorded in any book.

Yet for a camp that literally writes its history on its walls, there have been so far few attempts to tell its story from the beginning. This book is a modest attempt to do just that. Starting with the founding of Camp Ropioa, then continuing through the start of Camp Owatonna and up to the present, the following pages provide glimpses from each decade since 1922.

Clearly, much has changed in all those years—for example, comic books were contraband in the 1960s, Walkman cassette players in the 1980s, and smartphones in the present. What the reader will no doubt notice is that, in many ways, Camp has hardly changed. Owatonna, especially, still uses many of the procedures and activities that were established when it began in the 1950s and 1960s. While the routine at Ropioa was a bit less structured, its programming still feels familiar with its daily cabin inspection, intra-camp competitions, and even games of Gitchi-Gumi.

Steady since the beginning has been Camp's mission to nurture spiritual growth in both its campers and counselors. The highest aim at Ropioa was, of course, right there in its name—"reflection of perfection"—and the highlight of its weekly campfire meetings was testimonies of "progress in good." Similarly, the atmosphere at Owatonna is accurately captured in this excerpt from the 1966 Staff Handbook: "It is part of our philosophy that it is in meeting challenges, in setting forth goals and in accomplishing them that the camper learns to use his Christian Science practically."

As many of us will attest, Camp has been a unique proving ground for countless Christian Science healings and personal growth. Without a doubt, every summer since 1922 has brought forth a "permanent good" that stays with the fortunate few who have walked its grounds, long after we've left the shores of Long Lake. It is the hope of the author that through reading this record of Camp's history, the reader will, in a way, revisit their home away from home and remember some of that permanent good that lives within them.

J. R. Suber, July 2021
Camper, 2000, '01, '03, '05 (C.I.T.)
Counselor, 2006, '07, '08, '10

1922 The flagpole, Round House, and Lodge

Part I
CAMP ROPIOA

CAMP ROPIOA
HARRISON, MAINE

George A. Stanley, Founder of Ropioa

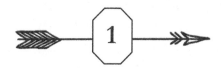

The history of Camp Owatonna begins with its predecessor Camp Ropioa—and Ropioa begins with its sister camp down the hill, Camp Newfound. As the story goes, George A. Stanley and his wife Gertrude came from New Jersey to visit Elizabeth Horton at Newfound. Mrs. Horton, known as "Aunt Elizabeth," founded Newfound in 1914 and was a close friend of the Stanleys. During the visit, Mrs. Horton suggested, "George, why don't you start a camp for boys? There is some beautiful property available adjacent to this." Mr. Stanley is said to have answered, "I've no more use for a boys' camp than a puppy has for two tails."[1] Regardless, Mr. Stanley did decide to purchase the property, and Camp ROPIOA, which stands for "Reflection Of Perfection Is Our Aim," opened in the summer of 1922.

George Stanley was an Englishman and about 50 years old when he started Ropioa. Known as Mr. Stanley to his campers, he was a "no-nonsense director" who ran a well-ordered camp, yet he managed—along with his wife Gertrude—to foster a deep affection from the counselors who worked for him.[2] One humorous anecdote provides a picture of Mr. Stanley:

Counselors and campers were expected to "toe the line." All of them could recall instances when [Stanley's] standard of excellence involved them. Bill Stevens [a Ropioa counselor during the 1930s] remembered when he was assigned to drive Mrs. Stanley into town for the mail. One letter slipped out between the seats and was overlooked. A day or so later, Mr. Stanley found it. That was Bill's last trip for the mail.[3]

Little is known about Mr. Stanley's background. Previous Camp histories described him as a retired British army officer who went by the title Colonel Stanley, but no information has been found to verify this.[4] Perhaps the most direct historical connection we have to Mr. Stanley is through Frank Hayden Connor, who was Mr. Stanley's Head Counselor in 1923. Connor recalled 50 years later that Stanley told stories about being in the British Army, and he described him as a "figure somewhat like 'John Bull'"—who is a British caricature equivalent to Uncle Sam in the United States.[5] Likewise, Allan White, a camper in 1934, records that during rainy nights in the Lodge, Mr. Stanley told stories about camping in the Sahara Desert and being chased by wolves through a Russian forest.[6] Phil Edwards, the second Director of Owatonna, said "Pop Stanley" was a big game hunter.[7] Were these facts about Mr. Stanley or just campfire tales?

A more dubious claim about Mr. Stanley is found in several accounts—including Connor's—that note that Stanley was the brother of Sir Henry Morton Stanley, the British explorer who famously tracked down Dr. David Livingstone in the African bush in 1871.[8] Although fascinating if true, the familial connection is doubtful for two reasons. First, Sir Henry Stanley was likely 30 years older than George Stanley, making him too old to be his sibling. Second, Sir Stanley was not really a "Stanley" at all—he was born John Rowlands and changed his name when he emigrated from England to the United States.

As for George Stanley, new research sheds some light on his origins. He was born in the late 1860s in England, likely 1869.[9] U.S. census records note that he immigrated to New Jersey in 1890, around the age of 21.[10] This timeline casts doubt on the notion that Stanley was a seasoned British army officer—he would have had to have joined as a teenager and served just a few years before moving to the United States. For what it's worth, Frank Hayden Connor recalled that after retiring from the army, Stanley developed a drinking problem. "He came to this country to start over and heard of Christian Science through which he had a healing."[11]

In 1895, around the age of 26, he married Ida May Eltringham, who was born and raised in Jersey City. By 1905, they were living in Ridgewood, New Jersey, and George's occupation was listed as a manager at a music box manufacturer.[12] Sadly, Ida passed away in 1908.[13] George stayed in Ridgewood, and later in 1914, he remarried New Jersey native, Gertrude R. Taylor.[14]

It is in large part through Gertrude that Ropioa came to be. According to Newfound history, Gertrude was close friends with Aunt Elizabeth, the founder of Camp Newfound.[15] The Stanleys and Hortons must have known each other because they all lived in Ridgewood—they probably attended the same Christian Science church. Gertrude is believed to have been a counselor at Newfound since its beginning, and she appears in several photos from its early years.[16] Interestingly, both Gertrude and George were listed as "retired" in the 1915 U.S. census, meaning they were perhaps looking for a new venture to occupy their time.[17] With all these facts combined, it is not surprising that the Stanleys would have been some of the first to know when the property bordering Camp Newfound went up for sale.

1930 George and Gertrude Stanley

The owner of the property at the time was Joseph S. Chaplin, a farmer and horseman who was born and raised in Harrison. His grandparents, Jane and Benjamin Chaplin, had first settled on nearby Plaisted Hill in the 1820s. Joseph was born in 1859.[18] Town records indicate he served as Secretary of the

Northern Cumberland Agricultural Society in 1890, as well as on the Board of Selectmen from 1897 to 1900.[19] Newspapers show he enjoyed participating in local horse shows.[20]

In 1908, Chaplin and his wife Hestildah purchased 125 acres of land from Luther C. Edwards.[21] The land had been a homestead farm since at least the 1860s and had passed through a number of owners since then.[22] The parcel of land stretched all the way from Naples Road down to Long Pond—now known as Long Lake—and it also included land east of the road, namely a rectangular field enclosed by a stone wall.[23] The Chaplins also came into possession of a small island—later known as Cherry Island—but they sold it in 1911 to their neighbor Charles E. Roberts.[24]

In 1916, Hestildah passed away, and within a few years, Chaplin put the farm up for sale.[25] It was around this time that Mr. and Mrs. Stanley must have made their visit to Camp Newfound and learned of the property.[26] On March 26, 1920, Chaplin signed the deed for the 125 acres over to the Stanleys.[27] The *Bridgton News* reported that the farm would be used as a camp adjoining Elizabeth Horton's Camp Newfound.[28] Chaplin continued to live in Harrison and Bridgton until he passed away in July 1931.[29]

1925 Mr. Stanley in the Lodge

THE STANLEY YEARS
(1922-34)

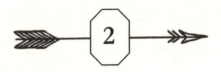

Ropioa's first summer of programming was likely in 1922. There are some indications of activity before then, but the record is sparse. Several months after purchasing the property in 1920, Stanley put out an advertisement in the *Bridgton News* listing as for sale four driving horses, one pony, a cart, and saddles.[30] These were perhaps assets that came with the Chaplin farm but were no longer needed. A year later in 1921, Stanley put out two more advertisements. He was looking to hire a cook who would feed eight to ten people in July and August for a salary of $100, as well as two young ladies who would wait on tables and clean rooms.[31] These two advertisements suggest that Ropioa possibly had campers there in 1921, but no other information has been found to corroborate this.

By 1922, however, Ropioa was operational.[32] Indeed, early advertisements inviting boys to enroll appeared in May and June 1922 in the *Christian Science Monitor*.[33] The ads read:

The success of CAMP NEWFOUND
for Girls has brought forth

Camp Ropioa
FOR BOYS

Beautiful for situation overlooking the White Mountains. A very large lodge and dining hall with most modern equipment, large screened tents afford comfortable sleeping quarters. Horse-back riding, archery, cricket, tennis, swimming, boating, canoeing, water polo, camping trips, mountain hikes, 125 acres of woodland. Half-mile lake frontage. Teachers all experts. Also camp for adult visitors.

GEORGE A. STANLEY
14 E Dayton St., Ridgewood, N.J.

There are at least three photos from that summer. One shows the very first all-camp photo.[34] In the middle stands Mr. Stanley, a middle-aged man with a receding hairline. He is wearing a white button-down shirt with a small bowtie and British knickerbockers. Flanking him are nine boys in shorts, mostly wearing dark blue tank tops with just two displaying the Ropioa logo.[35] Two counselors stand on either end, bringing the total number in the photo to 12—a modest beginning to Camp.

Two other photos show the campgrounds.[36] Notable are the Lodge, Director's cottage, and three sleeping tents—all in the same locations as today. The Lodge and cottage are slightly simplified but largely the same. It was said years later that the tents were believed to be old British explorer tents, perhaps connected to Mr. Stanley's mysterious past travels.[37] There are a few noteworthy differences from the grounds back then to what stands there today. Next to the flagpole, there was a gazebo structure—called the Round House—and a firepit. In place of the Birches and counselor cabin, there was a large farmhouse and barn, leftovers from the Chaplin farm.

Just 12 Ropioans and 125 acres of woodland—that's a lot of space to play in! Not much else is known about this first summer. However, based on the advertisements, there was plenty to do even in this first year of programming. Activities included horseback riding, archery, tennis, and boating.

The rest of what is known about the 1920s is mostly found in photographs and a couple of documents. A 1923 directory of American summer camps records Ropioa as having a staff of four, an enrollment of 15, and a tuition of $350.[38] The Head Counselor that summer was 21-year-old Frank Hayden Connor, a rower at Princeton, who would spearhead the founding of Camp Owatonna three decades later. After the summer, Mrs. Stanley wrote on behalf of her husband to Connor, thanking him for "the care so lovingly given to the boys in your charge."[39] Evidently, the Stanleys were still learning how best to operate the camp, as Mrs. Stanley suggests that next year counselors should stay after campers leave to help close down the property. "You can't imagine all there is to do, before and after—I guess the after is the worse," she writes, mentioning taking in docks, packing up books, scrubbing floors, and painting boats.[40]

By 1925, Camp had grown, as seen in several photographs. There were now seven sleeping tents in the grove to accommodate nearly 50 campers, and the staff had increased to 11.[41] Nearly all camper uniforms now featured the Ropioa logo on the chest. Mr. Stanley dressed in all white and wore his signature bowtie. Camp also had perhaps its first resident dog, a small cocker spaniel, seen curled up at the feet of the boys in two different photos.[42] One photo shows the early interior of the Lodge. All the boys and counselors are gathered around Mr. Stanley, who sits in front of the fireplace, appearing to be in the middle of some story.[43] Unlike today, the walls of the Lodge are quite barren, save for a few hanging photos; if you look closely, one of the photos is the all-camp photo from 1922, establishing a Lodge tradition that continues today.

A series of photographs from Kahill-Spratt Photo Studios, including a fantastic panorama, shows that there had been some fun additions to the grounds by 1928. The baseball diamond and Rec Hall were added. In between them were a riflery range and an unpaved basketball court. In the large open space that would eventually become Coomber Stadium, there was an archery target and a volleyball net. Continuing up the grassy hill from the Rec Hall, where the archery range is today, there were two enclosed grass tennis courts. Walking towards the flagpole, there was a third clay tennis court.

Finally, in the grove between the tents and the Lodge, there was a Native American totem pole, which stayed until at least 1940.[44] One of the most interesting photos from 1928 shows the entire camp gathered around the totem pole.[45] The younger boys sit in a semi-circle, while counselors stand in a line behind them. They are all dressed in Native American regalia—with feathered headbands and blankets draped around their shoulders. The boys look to have single feathers, while the counselors have multiple—a few with full-on war bonnets. Facing them on the other side of the totem pole is presumably Mr. Stanley, raising an arm and commanding their attention. The totem pole itself is covered in dozens of symbols, which reminiscences from later years explain were painted by each camper. Some of the markings include a handprint, a mountain, initials, and even a Masonic symbol.

As a historical note, caricatures of Native American cultures were common aspects of early American summer camps. This tendency reflected a broader "back-to-nature" movement that swept through the increasingly urbanized U.S. population in the late 19th century. Summer camps themselves originated out of this era as a way to give children, who were no longer needed as extra hands on the farm, something to do, and to get many out of the cities for a period of time. Thus, many summer camps adopted Native American-sounding names and embedded Native American-like elements into their programming. As one academic paper about the history of summer camps puts it:

> 'Indianness' was performed in multiple settings and through a variety of media, including pageantry, dance, ceremonies, woodcraft, games, and crafts.... Children slept in Indian villages, grew vegetables in Indian gardens, and held campfires and performed rights in the Indian council ring.[46]

Another photo from 1928 shows the entire camp inside the Lodge, likely meeting for Sunday School.[47] There look to be 11 groups of campers and counselors, all with sets of books in their laps. A piano is set up in the back corner. On the back wall behind Mr. Stanley hangs a massive U.S. flag. Interestingly, the flag only has 42 stars, which dates the flag to 1890, although there were 48 states by the time Camp Ropioa was established.

Who exactly these early campers and counselors were is mostly lost to history, but some names are mentioned in letters. For example, a February 1924 letter written by Mr. Stanley mentions that enrollments for the upcoming season were received from the Ford boys, little Lawrence, and Bob Rypinski. Additionally, and fortunately, a few early all-camp photos have names handwritten on them. Thus, we know in 1928 that a few campers included George Bagley, Len Webster, and Phil Sobel, and we also have a near-complete list of the staff that summer, the earliest known:

Mr. Franklin Emerson	Mr. Philips
Mr. David Jacobs	Mr. Watson
Mr. Tomson	Mr. Alan Barnes
Mr. Macinis	Mr. Norm Parseils
Mr. Gardner	Mr. Sullivan
Mr. Cloud	Mr. Al Romero
Mr. Mackay	Mr. Willis Lawrence
Mr. Don Lowe	Mr. John Cooper[48]

Mr. Romero and Mr. Cooper would later help establish Camp Owatonna; Mr. Lowe would eventually become Director of Ropioa. More than half of these counselors returned for the 1929 summer, and enrollment grew to nearly 60 campers. Some of the campers included Dick Coleman, Charles Edelman, Nat Hirsch, George Fink, Frank Meier, as well as returning old boys George Bagley and Len Webster.[49] A 1929 cabin photo from John Weil records his counselors as being Mr. Jacobs and Mr. Emerson, and his bunkmates as being Bob Crook, Mort Paul, Norbert Hoffman, and George Robinson.[50] Most of the campers were from the New England and Tri-state area. However, there was at least one traveler from afar in 1930—Robert "Bobby" Lane came all the way from Johannesburg, South Africa![51] The only thing of note about this final year of the 1920s is that by this summer Stanley had hired on extra help in the form of local residents Charles M. Bowser and his wife, also named Gertrude, who served respectively as camp caretaker and cook.[52]

1928 Sunday School in the Lodge

1928 An early Council Fire meeting

1929 Diving

1930s Canoeing to Raspberry Island, later called Cherry Island

1930s Bugler playing at flagpole

1928 Panorama of Ropica's grounds

Whereas our knowledge of Ropioa in the 1920s is mostly pieced together from photographs and obscure documents, we have more insight into Camp during the 1930s, due to several reminiscences and newsletters that provide long-forgotten details.

Hal Heim was a camper from 1932 to 1939. His reminiscence, written 60 years later, provides an overview of Ropioa that in many ways shows—aside from the screened tents—how little Camp has changed since then:

> We lived in screen tents with raised platforms, roll-down flaps, and a single lantern as tents were not electrified. Seven to a tent plus a counselor, and a footlocker or camp trunk next to each bed. We brought our own blankets. There were 7 or 8 tents, built around the side of a shaded hill.
>
> A typical day began with lining up at the flagpole near the Lodge at 7:30 A.M., and a bugler blew reveille as the flag was raised, rain or shine. On Sundays, the flag event was at 8:00 A.M., so we got to sleep in an extra half hour. Following breakfast, beds were made, floors swept, and inspected. Each tent earned points, and counselors motivated us with different carrot techniques, mostly to ensure they were given a day off each week. The day ended with blowing of Taps at 9:00 P.M., sometimes followed by reading magazines with flashlight, under the blankets.
>
> Camp dress consisted of blue serge shorts and sleeveless tops and sneakers, period. That was it, counselors included, except for a few special events, when they got to wear white ducks or flannels and campers wore white shirts (but no "big boy" pants), on Sunday only.[53]

Writing about the many available activities, Hal remembers the "untold hours of happiness, teamwork, discipline, competitiveness, 'can do' attitudes, and drain of untold energies."[54] There were week-long canoe trips, an annual hike up Mt. Pleasant, and trips to Harrison and North Bridgton. Of course, the most important activity was "eating lots of food...best described as 'gut fillers.'"[55] Occasional special treats included frozen Milky Ways and the New England soft drink Moxie.

One activity that Hal mentions was the bi-weekly newsletter titled the *Echo*. It was written and printed mostly by the campers and was full of short articles and cartoons. Fortunately, all the editions of the *Echo* from the summer of 1934 have survived, providing a fascinating record of eight weeks at Ropioa.

Activities were abundant: sports included swimming, baseball, football, riflery, archery, and tennis. Photography and woodshop were also available, and for the early risers there was fishing. Weekly canoe trips explored Long Lake and went as far as Sebago Lake for an overnight. Often, one canoe in the flotilla would be loaded up with a Victrola to blare merry melodies. For those who enjoyed a faster ride, there were motorboat trips in the "Margaret." Hiking was limited—the furthest being an overnight on Mt. Pleasant. A few times, the entire camp walked to Harrison and was treated to ice cream and soda.

There were no permanent teams at this point, but intra-camp competitions saw recurring team identities that varied by sport: Senior division baseball had the Tramps versus the Hoboes; Junior division baseball had the Loafers versus the Bums; riflery had the Poppers versus the Plunkers. Once a summer, there was a swim meet, as well as a track meet. Other all-camp activities included Tug of War, Capture the Flag, and a game called the Hare & Hound Chase, which perhaps was a combination of a scavenger hunt and tag.

One brand new game introduced this year by the counselor Mr. Breed was the Gitchi-Gumi Hunt, which occurred every other week. As described by camper Bob Trilsch—who later helped found Camp Owatonna—one tent would hide in the woods between the Boat Dock path and the Beach path. One member would carry the Gitchi, a block of wood. The rest of the camp were the Gumis, who went out to find the hiding campers. If the Gitchi was caught, then it was hung as a trophy in the tent of the camper who found him. In the very first Gitchi-Gumi Hunt, Len Webster crawled under Tent #10 with the Gitchi and was never caught.[56]

There were joint events with Camp Newfound nearly once a week. The first meeting with the girls in 1934 was a Fourth of July celebration at Ropioa. The girls arrived after dinner to roast marshmallows in the fireplace and set off sparklers, while older boys went down to the baseball field to set off flares.[57] Other co-ed activities that summer included a talent show, a musical concert, and a Christian Science lecture by Judge Samuel W. Green, of Chicago, Illinois, titled "Christian Science, the Religion of Joy."

The camps did Sunday School separately, and on Sunday evenings Ropioa held a Song Service, which essentially was a hymn sing. Another activity of the time was called Monitor Meeting, a weekly meeting during which campers would present brief summaries of articles from *The Christian Science Monitor*. One topic often covered that summer was advances in aviation—camper Ted Heller briefed everyone on the famous Kepner-Stevens stratosphere flight that occurred in July, in which three daring explorers climbed 60,000 feet in a balloon that then ruptured, forcing them to parachute to safety.[58]

The 1934 *Echo* newsletters also provide the earliest-known details about one of Camp's longest standing traditions: Council Fire. Back then, it was known as the P.G.T., or Pathway to Golden Truth. Hal Heim described it as so:

> This was a mystical Indian-oriented organization we all belonged to. At night, we donned a blanket, moccasins, and to the beat of a tom-tom, met at the one and only bathroom known as "The Perch," and proceeded down a rock-bound dirt path to a circular clearing in the woods, ringed with large flat rocks we sat on. Once every two weeks, white, red, and blue feathers were awarded for accomplishments. These were worn in a headband. Initiation into P.G.T. included eating a piece of bear meat (no doubt some leftover pot roast) and drinking water from a well-known Indian Reservation (probably right out of Long Lake). Gathered around a small fire, we listened to stories, sang and spoofed one another.[59]

The meetings were typically held on Friday nights almost on a weekly basis. In 1934, it seems that the meeting was moved from its original location "under the Bent Pine" to a new council ring, although there are no details that specify where exactly these places were.

Every camper and counselor required initiation into the "tribe," which required passing various tests and taking an oath. Hal mentions eating and drinking as part of the initiation, but other examples include not being allowed to talk during weekly activities like Tug of War, as well as fasting and "watching alone" in the P.G.T. council ring.

When counselors gained initiation, they became "chiefs" and received a Native American-inspired name, some examples being Chief Strong Arm, Chief Hawk Eye, and Chief Red Cloud. The emcee of the event was always Chief Great Wisdom, who was likely Mr. Stanley, and his deputy was Chief Black Feather.

Everyone sat in a ring around the council fire. The meeting opened and closed with prayers of thanks to "Woconda of the Four Winds" and to the "Great Spirit." After the testing and initiation of new members, feather awards were granted to campers for various achievements from the week. Then, there was time for the sharing of stories, gratitude, and testimonies. Chief Great Wisdom might share some thoughtful words, and then the fire would be extinguished, and the campers would retire to their tents "with the spell of the meeting still upon them."[60]

The totem pole was an important feature of the P.G.T., as well. In the first two weeks of the 1934 summer, boys added their markings to the pole. David Altrock left his initials, Russell Clifton painted a propeller plane, and Bertram Williams left an "amusing gray animal which, though intended for a monkey, greatly resembles a pelican."[61] The totem pole was then raised up in a P.G.T. ceremony on a Saturday morning. The boys were again all dressed in their Native American garb, but this time they welcomed Camp Newfound to witness the event. The totem was meant to be a special way for campers to leave their marks at Camp. The counselor Mr. Breed noted its deeper meaning when he mused, "Even as each of us has left his mark upon this pole, so may Ropioa leave its mark on us in enabling us to carve out grand and noble characters that men may behold the results of our application of all that is good and true."[62]

As noted previously, the incorporation of Native American cultures into Ropioa programming reflected a common practice among early American summer camps at the time, which persisted throughout most of the 20th century. A noteworthy observation is that Ropioa made some effort to learn about authentic Native American traditions, rather than merely caricature them. For example, in 1934 Ropioa and Newfound spent an evening watching educational motion picture videos about Native American customs and religious ceremonies. These were reels taken in 1912 of the Pueblo, Navajo, and Hopi tribes, and they showed pottery making, basketry, and life in the home, as well as the nine-day-long Hopi snake dance. "We all felt that the evening was well spent," wrote Bob Trilsch, "and all of us came away with a little more understanding of the Indian tribes of the Southwest."[63]

Additionally, Hal Heim remembers that every summer Penobscot Indians would visit Ropioa. The Penobscot tribe was and remains one of the largest in New England. Their protected reservation is located along the Penobscot River near Bangor, Maine. According to Heim, the Indians "dressed in full regalia, performed dance ceremonies, and we were in awe." They apparently also helped the Ropioans raise their totem pole.[64] More details of these visitors were recorded by counselor Bill Stevens in the *Echo* newsletter. On Saturday, July 28, Princess Wattawasso and her husband Chief Poolaw came to Camp. Wattawasso—an annual visitor to Ropioa according to Stevens—brought baskets and handicrafts to sell. Her husband, a Kiowa Indian from Oklahoma who dressed in a buffalo headdress, sang Kiowa war songs for the kids. "We were all glad the Chief was our friend and not on the warpath," recorded the *Echo*.

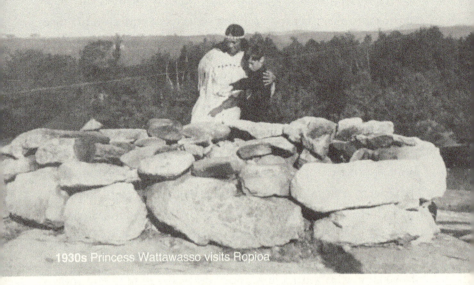

1930s Princess Wattawasso visits Ropioa

Princess Wattawasso's real name was Lucy Nicolar Poolaw, and her husband was Bruce Poolaw. She was a somewhat-famous Penobscot woman who had performed around the country for years on what was known as the Chautauqua lecture circuit. A classically trained singer, her performances involved dressing in Native American garb and singing both Native American and classical songs. She was also known as a political activist. For example, she gained early recognition when in 1900, as a 17-year-old, she spoke up at a public debate on immigration and was quoted as saying that she was the only "true American here."[65] As described in the *Echo*, "One has only to speak to her to be instantly aware of the presence of a woman of breeding and culture."[66] She met her husband during her touring, and together they opened a store in Maine that sold Native American wares.

The 1934 summer ended with a festive banquet. "As usual, the tables were arranged in horseshoe formation, and were adorned with flowers and ferns, and the rafters with boughs. Mr.

and Mrs. Stanley sat at the center of the table forming the bend of the horseshoe, with the boys and counsellors along the sides." The menu was hearty: roast turkey, mashed potatoes, corn on the cob, and hot biscuits; for dessert there was ice cream, two different cakes, candy, and an assortment of fruits.

This was also when awards were handed out for various achievements from the summer. The most prestigious award was the naming of the "R" camper, which was given to the best all-round camper. The "R" was an actual letter fastened to the winner's uniform. George Bagley, Jr. had won the "R" back in 1933.[67] And then the banquet closed with remarks from Mr. Stanley, marking the completion of the summer:

> When the dishes were cleared away, Mr. Stanley arose and expressed his gratitude to the divine Love that made Camp Ropioa possible, and for His guidance and protection. Then he thanked Mrs. Stanley and the counsellors for their co-operation, and the boys for the good spirit which they had taken part in the various camp activities.[68]

George and Gertrude Stanley apparently semi-retired after the 1935 summer. There has been some confusion about what happened to the Stanleys next. Most camp histories state that Mr. Stanley passed away in the 1930s, leaving Mrs. Stanley to run the camp.[69] However, the records indicate that Mr. Stanley lived until 1947 and Mrs. Stanley until 1959. In fact, they seem to have maintained some involvement in Ropioa for the next several years because they continued to appear in camp photos. Running the camp in their place was a new and young Christian Scientist couple.

1930s Ropioa campers lived in screened-in tents

1930s The Ropioa beach

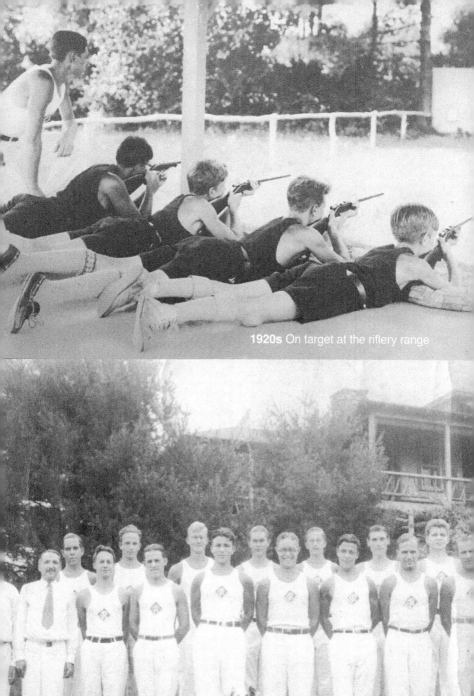

1920s On target at the riflery range

1930 Ropioa counselors

1930s Ropioa grounds

1939 Don Lowe as Director

THE LOWE YEARS
(1935-40)

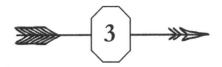

In August 1935, the Stanleys sold Ropioa to Don and Enid Lowe for $50,000.[70] Don Lowe was a native Mainer, born in 1903 in Lewiston, but he grew up in Swampscott, Massachusetts.[71] He graduated from Philips Exeter Academy in 1923, where he was described in the yearbook as "sober, steadfast, and demure."[72] He later graduated from Dartmouth and spent the next five years teaching, including a year at Harvard University. In 1932 he became headmaster at the Winnwood School on Long Island.[73] A year later, he married Enid Goss, a Christian Scientist from Toronto, and they made their home first on Cape Cod and then in Swampscott (just a quarter mile from where Mary Baker Eddy had lived in the 1860s).[74]

Don Lowe was advertised as the new Director of Ropioa in a 1936 ad in the *Christian Science Monitor*, and he and Enid ran Camp until at least 1939.[75] Don's first year as a counselor had been in 1926, and he appears to have been a regular from then on.[76] He is visible in the 1927 all-camp photo—in which he is holding the camp bugle—as well as in photos from 1929 and 1931.

Camper Hal Heim remembers the transition from Mr. Stanley to Mr. Lowe, who was 33 years old at the time, significantly younger than his predecessor. He was "more congenial and, because of age perhaps, [we] found it easier for us to communicate with [him]."[77]

Some good detail from the Lowe years is drawn from 1938 and 1939 Newfound newsletters, which share tidbits about co-ed activities with their Ropioa neighbors. One dispatch from June 1938 reports:

> Twenty little Newfounders all dressed up, done in style, to attend the first semi-formal dance given by their brother camp, Ropioa. We had a hearty welcome by our hosts who looked quite striking in their coats and neckties. Programs were given out and we started the evening off with a grand march.... Everyone looked most attractive, and had the boys going some to keep up with them. Ten o'clock came all too soon for us, and we very sadly bid adieu to our gracious hosts, and came home bubbling with the excitement of our first dance at Ropioa — minus the camp uniforms.[78]

Other co-ed activities that year included a variety show—featuring Mr. Lowe at the piano—theater performances, a tennis tournament, and a baseball game between "Rofound" and "Nupioa," documented as so:

> Ropioa's best sluggers were warming up for the big event with the fair damsels, who by the way were "ready, willing, and able" to strike at something. Rofound, alias Patty's men, were up at bat first, while Nupioa spread out all over the lot awaiting that familiar utterance "batter up!" which was to start the game — the first of the season between Newfound

and Ropioa. The shower passed over our heads and lasted just long enough to scatter the players and the cheering sections to the rifle range and a grove of trees, and to give the ball and grass a good soaking. As everybody discovered, there was nothing like playing with a soggy ball, but by the end of the seventh inning with Rofound winning with a score of 9 — 3, the game was called and the ball thoroughly dried out.[79]

Write-ups from the following summer in 1939 included descriptions of many similar joint activities, as well as this summary of the Fourth of July celebration down at Newfound:

A red, white and blue surprise awaited us as we entered the dining room the night of the 4th.... That evening feminine hearts beat fondly as Ropioa made its 1939 debut on the Newfound grounds.... A bonfire and sparklers awaited us all down at the point, and new romances showed signs of sprouting and old ones of continuing. We are now wondering about a triangle concerning a certain blond Ropioan and guess who.[80]

Other joint activities in 1939 included the usual tennis and baseball matches, but also rainy-day games in the Ropioa Lodge and hymn sings on Sunday nights.

Photographs indicate a few changes that took place through the 1930s. The uniform adopted the use of white short-sleeved shirts sometimes worn under the dark blue Ropioa tank top. The Lodge's exterior was painted a very light color, perhaps light green as can be seen on the wall inside the Camp Mom's office today. The canvas tents were upgraded to have real roofs and more substantial siding. Finally, the Round House may have been removed around this time—at least one photo seems to show it missing from the flagpole area.

In December 1939, the Lowes sold their share of Camp back to the Stanleys for unknown reasons.[81] Although in his late 30s, Don may have gone on to serve in World War II, as there is a record of his draft card (which notes he was 5'6", 176 lb., and a teacher at Swampscott High School).[82] By 1944, the Lowes were living in Los Angeles but soon after took up teaching positions at Rutgers University.[83]

In January 1940, just a few weeks after the transaction with the Lowes, the Stanleys put an advertisement in the *Christian Science Monitor* listing camp equipment for sale, foreshadowing changes ahead. However, there was still one more final summer of programming in 1940.

It's unknown who exactly ran the camp this year. Perhaps this was the summer that Gertrude Stanley did much to operate Ropioa herself, as previous Camp histories suggest. Bill Rupp was a camper there in 1940, and he recalls the Director was a man named Meyers who only ran the camp for that one year and with the help of several family relatives. Perhaps it was Frank Meyer, a counselor during the Lowe years.[84]

Rupp provides a few more details from that summer. He was a 13-year-old from New Jersey, and this was the only summer he attended Ropioa. He was in Tent #4, and one of his counselors was former camper Hal Heim. He remembers that Heim kept a portable Victrola record player in the tent; Heim would play Glenn Miller records while humorously dancing with the center pole of the tent as his partner. Another memory Rupp has is when Camp was visited by a truck shaped like a soda bottle. All the campers received a free bottle of Moxie; he took one swig and then felt compelled to pour the rest out on the ground![85]

Rupp also remembers there was a Ropioa hymn that all the boys sang. He can still recall the words 80 years later:

> Yes, Ropioa is our name
> We boys, too, will be true to the same
> And try in all things to achieve
> The joy of Love we all believe
> In all things, be the best at our game
> Reflection of Perfection Is Our Aim

The 1940 summer was by most accounts the last for Camp Ropioa as a place for Christian Science boys. That November, the Stanleys sold the camp for $30,000 to John LaMarsh of New York, who kept the Ropioa name but made the camp non-denominational. It's not clear exactly why the Stanleys sold the camp. Previous histories incorrectly believed that Mr. Stanley's passing contributed to Mrs. Stanley's decision to sell; however, now it is known that Mr. Stanley lived well into the 1940s. Frank Hayden Connor, who would later help start Owatonna, believed economic difficulties lingering from the Great Depression may have contributed.[86] Sally Manley, the wife of future Owatonna Trustee Al Romero, thought that the beginning of World War II may have been a factor, yet the United States wouldn't enter the war until the end of 1941. Regardless, she recalls that her husband Al and fellow Ropioa counselor Bill Stevens helped shut down the camp on behalf of the Stanleys.[87]

Although Ropioa continued in name, this change in ownership marked the end of one camp and the start of another, which John LaMarsh operated for the next 15 years. As for the Stanleys, they appear to have moved by 1944 from Ridgewood,

New Jersey, to Niantic, Connecticut, a small village on the Atlantic coast.[88] A few years later in 1947, George Stanley passed away.[89] Gertrude would live on to see the creation of Camp Owatonna a decade later, formed by former Ropioa counselors. In fact, she would become a helpful supporter when that time came. She remained close to Owatonna, as indicated by the fact that she received an invitation in 1958 to attend the end-of-summer banquet as a special guest.[90] She politely declined but wished the young camp her best. Gertrude passed away the following year.[91]

1930s Ropioa campers and counselor

INTERIM YEARS
(1941-55)

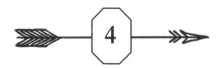

Not much is known about John LaMarsh's Camp Ropioa. It was advertised as a Christian camp, and its first season was in 1941.[92] It did not associate with Camp Newfound at all during these interim years, making the boys up the hill a bit mysterious to their co-ed neighbors. Anne Wold, a future Newfound Director who was a young camper in the 1940s, remembers that one time a Newfound boat drifted over to the Ropioa beach, and they had to send a delegation over to help get it back. When the girls returned, all were very interested in hearing what it was like "over there."[93]

Some details are gleaned from a 1954 issue of the Ropioa Review. There was swimming, boating, and sports. Inter-camp games were played against Winona, O-AT-KA, Takajo, and Wigwam. Staples like Capture the Flag, scavenger hunts, and Hounds n' Hares were played across the campgrounds.[94]

Riflery and horseback riding were still available. In fact, Newfound may have shared the riding facilities in the early 1940s, because after 1943 they began taking lessons from Mr.

Steve Burns, who lived in the farmhouse near the entrance to Ropioa.[95]

At the time, LaMarsh was also the Secretary of the Junior Maine State Guide Committee, so there was a strong emphasis on integrating Junior Maine Guides programming at Ropioa. This included sending campers for four days to pass various JMG tests at a site on the Rangeley Lakes. Campers also took trips out to Sebago Lake, Mount Chocorua, and North Conway—some even went on a four-day trip all the way in Quebec!

It's not known whether there was any kind of Council Fire, although the newsletter does mention conducting a Song Fest in the Council Ring. Mr. LaMarsh was affectionately referred to as "Chief" LaMarsh. An inventory list from 1952 records that there were "Indian lore" items stored in the Lodge at this time, and that there were two Council Rings.[96]

Instead of interacting with the girls at Newfound, Ropioa visited Camp Tawasi down the road. Tawasi was run by John LaMarsh's wife, Irene, and it had been established earlier in 1933, at some point moving onto the old Camp Wyonee property.[97]

As for Newfound, they found new opportunities for socializing. Sometimes, they would go to socials with the boys of Long Lake Lodge, located on the other side of the lake. The Lodge was a summer tutoring school for boys, established in 1902 and in operation until around 1985.[98]

Additionally, Newfound would also meet up with boys from Camp Passaconaway, a local camp that attracted a contingent of Christian Science boys after Ropioa changed ownership. It was a Christian camp, established in 1909 on Bear

Island in Lake Winnipesaukee in New Hampshire, but in 1932 it relocated to McWain Pond in Waterford, Maine.[99] The longtime Directors were Arthur Godfrey Carlson and his wife Mary. As early as 1933, Passaconaway advertisements began appearing in the *Christian Science Monitor,* so Christian Scientists would have been aware of it before the closure of Ropioa.[100]

At some point between 1943 and 1948, Christian Scientists Claude Lourie Hough and his wife Martha became the Directors of Passaconaway.[101] Although the camp was advertised as "non-sectarian," the number of Christian Science boys had grown sizeable by the 1950s.[102] A 1953 enrollment and staff list notes that there were 52 Christian Scientists.[103] Co-ed activities with Newfound were a natural match and included dances as well as joint Sunday School classes.

David Youngblood was a camper at Passaconaway in 1954, and he remembers being the youngest boy in the oldest cabin. One of his cabinmates, he recalls, was an exuberant fellow whose favorite song was the 1920s-era Jimmie Rodgers song "I'm in the Jailhouse Now," which the boy sang often and piercingly.[104] Another memory he has is of paying C.I.T.s one night to bring back ice cream from their night off. He was woken from a sound sleep to a pint of slightly soupy ice cream that he ate by flashlight.[105] Youngblood would attend Owatonna when it opened a couple years later, and Passaconaway, having lost its core Christian Scientist constituency, would shut down by 1960.[106]

Back at Ropioa in these interim years, John LaMarsh began to run into trouble. In 1948, three cabins suffered fire damage, and in 1950 the old Joseph Chaplin farmhouse and barn burned down completely.[107] Although he formally paid off his mortgage to Gertrude Stanley in February 1952, LaMarsh had been taken to court by multiple entities the previous year.[108] And then, in 1953, he was hit with a series of tax liens for failure to pay taxes on Ropioa and Tawasi, which reoccurred every year through 1959.[109] In March 1952, LaMarsh took out another mortgage on Ropioa for $25,000 from New Yorker Benjamin DeMascola.[110] Two years later, on September 30, 1954, a public notice appeared in the *Bridgton News* announcing that DeMascola was foreclosing on LaMarsh, thereby assuming ownership of the Ropioa property.[111]

An opportunity thus presented itself, and so it was at this time that a group of Christian Scientists who had been Ropioa campers and counselors came together, united by the idea of purchasing the camp.

1950s Cartoons from the *Echo* newsletter

Part II
Camp Owatonna

1960s Flagpole

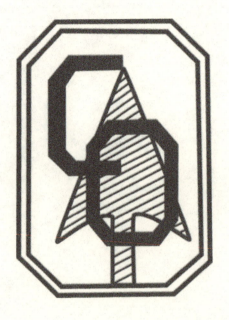

Founding Camp Owatonna (1955)

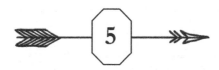

The sale of Camp Ropioa by Benjamin DeMascola was a topic of conversation at Camp Newfound's Parents Weekend in August 1955. According to a camp newsletter written a few years later, it was Al Romero who "sparked the imagination of several other Camp Ropioa alumni" when he suggested they find a way to reactivate the camp.[112] Romero had been a counselor and Head Counselor at Ropioa, where his fondness for canoeing earned him the affectionate title of "Admiral." In 1940, he had helped shut Ropioa down. Now, he wanted to help reopen it.

Another key alumnus got involved by way of his daughter. Frank Hayden Connor had been Mr. Stanley's Head Counselor in 1923. He went on to graduate from Princeton and was now the president of Carl Fischer, Inc., a successful music publishing company based in New York City.[113] His daughter Phoebe Ann Connor had grown up spending her summers at Newfound, likely often hearing stories from her father's years at Ropioa. In 1955, she was the Head Counselor under Newfound Director Dorothy Horton Cobb, known as "Becky." According to Frank, his daughter phoned to tell him that Ropioa was on the market.[114]

Details about what exactly happened next are not known, but it is apparent that all these individuals came together quickly, setting things in motion within three months. In November, the Newfound Camp for Boys Association was incorporated. Seven made up its first Board of Trustees. Frank Hayden Connor was named chairman and Al Romero vice-chairman. Serving as secretary was Becky and as treasurer was Boyd N. Jones, Jr. There was also John McGill Cooper, Jr., and William Robert Trilsch, Jr., both former Ropioa campers.[115] The final member, an active support from her retirement home in Niantic, Connecticut, was Gertrude Stanley.[116]

The sale of Ropioa was finalized a few months later in January 1956. DeMascola agreed to sell the property for $30,000, of which two-thirds would be paid out in annual installments over ten years.[117] Before the paperwork was even completed, planning for the next summer had already begun. As early as August 1955, Becky and Phoebe Ann Connor had started putting together lists of former Ropioa campers who might now have children of their own eligible for enrollment.[118] Camper lists from Passaconaway going back nearly ten years were obtained in order to identify the Christian Scientists who might find a new home at Ropioa.[119]

In mid-November, Frank Connor, his wife Phoebe, and Becky toured the property to survey necessary repairs and renovations, of which there were many—the roof on the Lodge needed re-shingling and ten cabins needed new roofs. They estimated that $8,000 was needed to complete the work before the summer. "This seems like a big amount to raise in a short time," wrote Frank, before following with, "As each step has unfolded so harmoniously, we know this will too."[120]

Public announcements advertising the upcoming 1956 summer began appearing in November and December. One in the *Christian Science Monitor* reads:

> Newfound sends a MERRY CHRISTMAS Greeting to its alumnae in many lands and takes this occasion to announce the reactivating of its former brother camp, located on the property adjoining. This camp was founded in 1922 under the name of Camp Ropioa by Mr. and Mrs. George A. Stanley, and operated by them through 1938 as a camp for boys from Christian Science homes. The reactivated boys camp will be owned by a non-profit corporation organized by several of its original councilors, and will be under the direct supervision of Camp Newfound.[121]

Inquiries were directed to Becky. She and Phoebe Ann Connor, who was in the middle of her studies at Vassar College, continued to work away at building a staff and enrolling campers.[122] Their correspondence shows that by February they had secured counselor commitments for every activity area except riflery. Enrollment proved more challenging, numbering just 27 boys by April. There also was the question of who would be the new Director of Ropioa. Letters show that by February, Frank Connor had secured a commitment from Tom Hilton to take on the role.

A native Michigander, Hilton was a seasoned camper and counselor from Camp Leelanau, a Christian Science camp in Leelanau County, Michigan. Similar to Ropioa, Leelanau had been established as a camp for boys in the early 1920s. With its emphasis on sports, outdoorsmanship, and even Native

American lore, Leelanau resembled much of Ropioa's programming. Becky and the Connors met with Hilton to "talk shop," and Becky was "very happily impressed with him and his background of knowledge about camping.... He is very simple and unassuming—and at first does not make any very outstanding impression on you—but he seems to 'grow on you.'"[123]

Hilton's experience at Leelanau made him a good fit to lead Ropioa for its reopening year. In the early 1950s, Hilton had worked as Leelanau's Head Counselor; he became Assistant Director in 1955.[124] A sense of Hilton's personality is captured in a quote from one of his camper friends who said of him, "After God, people came first in Tom Hilton's life.... He understood and communicated the satisfaction to be gained in giving of one's self in order to make some other person's life a little better."[125] Hilton was 35 years old when he came to Ropioa in 1956, and he brought his two boys, Tom Jr. and Dick, along with him for the summer.

The final change that needed to happen before the grand reopening of Camp Ropioa was to change the name "Ropioa." Using the name had become somewhat problematic by May 1955. Although John LaMarsh had lost the camp property to foreclosure, he still intended to reopen a new camp under the same name, and he went so far as to have his lawyer inform Frank Connor and the rest of the Trustees.[126] A rebranding, however, was a welcome idea, as debt collectors were still showing up at the camp property. A new name would more clearly disassociate them from LaMarsh's legal issues.[127] Frank Connor tells what happened next:

> This presented the proposition of finding a new name. We searched all the Maine and other New England Indian

names and found that most of them were already being used. One evening, in discussing it with the family, my wife's mother suggested, "Why don't you use the name of the town where you were born? Isn't that an Indian name?" We liked the idea and looked up the name to find that it was a Sioux Indian name meaning "straight," so we started to use the name and adopted the slogan for the boys: "Straight as an Arrow."[128]

Announcing the change, new Director Tom Hilton wrote to all the parents before the summer began. "You will be interested to know we have dropped the former name of 'Ropioa' in favor of a new name 'Owatonna' (O-wa-tonna, after the Sioux Indian word meaning 'straight')."[129] Thus, Camp Ropioa became Camp Owatonna, named after Owatonna, Minnesota, the town where Frank Connor had been born in 1902. Although his family moved away when he was just three years old, and he returned only once decades later, Frank felt that Maine and Minnesota both shared that special "something" that draws people from all parts of the country, at least for the summer.[130]

1950s Lining up for lunch

1950s Tom Hilton at Camp Leelanau

First Summer with Tom Hilton (1956)

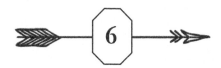

As for the actual first summer of Camp Owatonna, few details have survived beyond what activities were advertised and the names of staff and campers who were there. In fact, since most of the plaques in the Lodge begin their record-keeping in 1957, it has largely been forgotten that there was a 1956 summer. From a brochure, it is known that camp was still eight weeks long, running from Tuesday, June 26 to Tuesday, August 21. Tuition was listed at $450, although records indicate that scholarships were available and were awarded to six families in 1956.[131]

Activities included all the usual sports, as well as riflery, a new archery range, and horseback riding. Additionally, there was woodworking, arts and crafts, and band, which likely featured guitar playing. Outdoors trips included canoeing the Songo River into Sebago Lake, hikes through the White Mountains, and climbing Mt. Washington. On Sundays, there was joint Sunday School with Newfound.[132]

Tradition and competition have always been a core part of Owatonna ever since this first summer. Intra-camp teams were actually a common feature of American summer camps. One history of Maine summer camps refers to it as Color War and gives several examples:

> At Camp Wigwam, the campers were divided into the Red and Gray teams. At Camp Walden, the campers were either on the Brown team or the Tan team. Tripp Lake Camp, in Poland, divided campers into four teams along the same principles. Color War gave campers the chance to be part of a team, to express team spirit, and to engage in friendly competitions. Additionally, Color War gave some campers the opportunity to be leaders.[133]

According to Phil Edwards—who would become the next Director of Owatonna—it was Tom Hilton in 1956 who "initiated some of the same Indian lore and team organizations at Owatonna as were used at Leelanau."[134] Hilton had spent many years at Camp Leelanau, which featured both a Native American-themed weekly Council Fire and a three-team competition. The three teams at Leelanau were the Red Wolves, the Blue Eagles, and the Green Bears.[135] For Owatonna, Hilton kept the team colors but changed the names. As Edwards explained, "Tom utilized local Indian names to form three teams: the REDS became the Shawsheens; the BLUES, the Penobscots; and the GREENS, the Pequawkets."[136]

As Edwards stated, the names of the teams were apparently taken from local Native American places and tribes, although the exact origins are not entirely known. Research in *Native American Placenames of the United States* indicates that *Shawsheen* may come from the Shawsheen River in Essex County, Massachusetts. The river is supposedly named after a local

Algonquin man, who was known as Shoshanim or Sagamore Sam.[137]

As for the Greens, there is a Pequawket Pond in Oxford County, Maine, which is derived from *pigwacket,* an Abenaki word that means "land of hollows."[138] The Pequawket were a tribe that belonged to the Algonquin family of Native Americans and the Abenaki confederacy, which populated most of the region that makes up modern-day New England. Having been pushed from New Hampshire to Nova Scotia, the Pequawket fought and were defeated by the British in Lovewell's War in 1725. During the American Revolution from 1775 to 1783, however, the Pequawket allied with their former British enemies against the colonists. After defeat, they settled down in Quebec, Canada, but little more is known about the Pequawket as a distinct tribe.[139]

More well-known is the Penobscot tribe. Close relatives of the Pequawket, the Penobscot made up the "largest and most powerful tribe of the Eastern Abenaki."[140] They resided mostly in Maine, and their reservation is still located in the region. Their name in Algonquin, *benapskak,* means "at down-sloping rocks" and is likely a reference to where they lived.[141] Early maps of the New World attribute a large kingdom to the Penobscot, although this was found later to be largely inaccurate. During the American Revolution, they fought alongside the colonists and notably guided and took part in Benedict Arnold's 1775 assault on Quebec. Since the 18th century, however, the Penobscot have been marginalized by multiple treaties that gave away their lands in Maine and Massachusetts. By the 20th century, the tribal population had severely decreased and their language all but disappeared. They were awarded $81.5 million in 1980 by President Jimmy Carter as reparation for the U.S. government's previous predatory behavior. Today the Penobscot live on a 4,440-acre reservation located along the Penobscot River in Maine. Their community is slowing redeveloping and was estimated to have a population of approximately 2,000 in 1991.[142]

How much of this Native American history was known to Tom Hilton when he incorporated it into Owatonna's first summer is not known. Hilton likely drew most of the traditions that he implemented from his experiences at Camp Leelanau.

Camper and staff lists reveal who exactly took part in this first Owatonna summer. There were 36 campers, the two youngest being eight-year-olds Richard Berger and Ira Bartelstone, the oldest being 15-year-old David Youngblood. A significant number of them had been Passaconaway campers, such as Youngblood, Robert Petitmermet, Gordie Jones, and Dickie Vandervoort. Most were there for the full two months, although five were only enrolled for one month. Counselors, too, had come over from Passaconaway, such as Bill Birdsall, Jimmy Day, and Ty Anderson, who would later become a Director of Owatonna.[143]

A few details about this summer come from David Youngblood, who remembers that Owatonna felt like a "building project" when they arrived:

> All of us, campers, counselors, staff, were part of the enormous project of getting the camp re-built. I remember what a mess the boat dock was, how much the ballfields had to be reconstructed, how the rifle range was half-weeds, the basketball court a rutted combination of clay, dirt, and pebbles. There was one tennis court, and it had been

reclaimed pretty well. We had few of the amenities of later years, but roughing it, somehow, was more attractive.[144]

The camaraderie felt through this rebuilding effort made it perhaps "the golden year of Owatonna," says Youngblood. He thinks Ty Anderson was his counselor that year, who was in his view the ideal Owatonna man—a "combination of Flash Gordon, the Lone Ranger, and Mark Trail."[145] Youngblood remembers the general morning routine involved reveille, flagpole, breakfast, and cabin inspection. One more humorous anecdote from Youngblood is about a wilderness trip he went on:

> I went to the manager's office and made a request to call home. I wanted to go on the Lost River Trip. Everybody was going on the Lost River Trip! It was leaving in a few days, the cost was extra, and my family had said absolutely no extras. What a great name for a tourist attraction! What a great name for a trip! I had to go, and was reduced to tears and whimpering and, probably, extravagant promises to get my family to agree.[146]

The Lost River, located in Franconia Notch State Park, turned out to be an underwhelming almost-waterfall. Youngblood recalls the trip was "OK, a bit of a rip-off, but educational to the degree that whenever I saw other attractions later in life as I was driving around the country, I knew they were going to be mostly phony and show you 10%, at best, of what they promised."[147]

As for the summer overall, "it was a happy and successful season," according to a letter from the Board of Trustees.[148] For Tom Hilton, this was to be his only summer as Director at Owatonna, but it was not the end of his camping involvement.

He returned to Camp Leelanau in 1958 to be the Director there, a position he held well into the 1980s. At the same time, he was also a longtime educator at the Leelanau School.[149] As a tribute to Hilton's many years of service, Camp Leelanau established the "Tom Hilton Award" in the 1990s, which is given to one camper each summer who best represents the qualities of camp.[150] Hilton would, however, return to Owatonna as a special guest to celebrate its 10-year anniversary in 1966.[151] As it turned out, the next Director of Owatonna was a close friend of Hilton and was also a Leelanau man.

1956 Tom Hilton leading an off-camp excursion

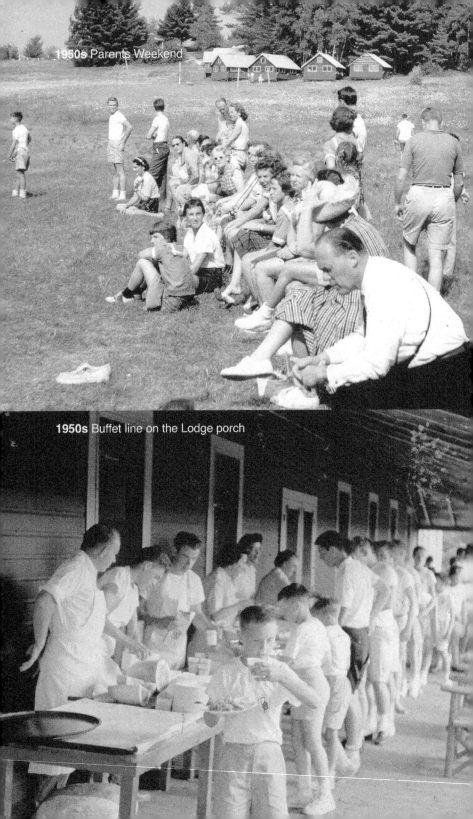

1950s Running up to flagpole

1950s Flagpole

1950s Catch of the day

1950s Hot meal in the Lodge

1950s The Boat House and Beach

1950s Cooking after a day of canoeing

1961 Reggie Browne, Ty Anderson, Doc Singer, Phil Edwards, Don Bliss

THE EDWARDS YEARS
(1957-63)

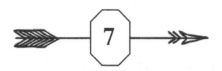

Following Hilton's departure, Phil Edwards was hired to be Owatonna's Director, as seen in this February 1957 advertisement in the *Christian Science Monitor:*

CAMP OWATONNA
ON LONG LAKE   HARRISON, MAINE

OFFERS BOYS

From Christian Science Homes a Happy, Active Summer
Beautiful Location
Modern Equipment
Expert Supervision
Experienced Counselors Provide the Best in Leadership and Guidance

For further information write to:

PHIL EDWARDS, DIRECTOR
CAMP OWATONNA, HARRISON, MAINE

Edwards was a 1941 graduate of Principia College, where he was an exceptional athlete. He was a forward in basketball, quarterback in football, and pitcher in baseball. He had pitched two perfect games while at Principia, which earned him offers to play professionally for the St. Louis Cardinals and the Chicago Cubs. He turned down both offers, however, in order to serve as a Naval officer, just as the United States entered World War II. At some point before Owatonna, Edwards worked as a counselor at Camp Leelanau, where he knew Tom Hilton.[152] Ultimately, he became an educator. He joined the English faculty at Principia Upper School in 1947, where he also coached basketball, football, and baseball. By 1965, he was the Assistant Headmaster, working under Englishman Eric Bole, who was himself an accomplished athlete.[153]

Edwards's background in education and coaching made him an ideal candidate for the Director role, a position he held for the next seven years, through the 1963 season. David Youngblood was a C.I.T. during Edwards's first summer, and he remembers him as a "steel gray-headed guy, hair in a crew cut, the very model of a modern ex-Marine. You wouldn't use empathetic words to describe him, but he was probably perfect for his office at that time: trim, a hard worker, pressed uniform, strong in his faith."[154]

As Director, Edwards built upon the organizational framework that Tom Hilton had laid out. He continued the core programs of activities, camping trips, and team competition, but he also implemented new ideas that became defining features of Owatonna. Start with the Lodge, where today the walls are adorned in dozens of colorful plaques that record generations of camper awards. Edwards created a robust point system for teams and campers to accumulate points through competitions, work projects, and individual achievements.[155]

As shown on the plaques and reported in the *Echo* newsletter, the Blues, captained by C.I.T. Terry Swanson, were victorious in the 1957 summer with 6,564 total points. Following them were the Greens with 5,934 points, then the Reds with 4,371 points.[156] Terry Swanson was "hands-down the best athlete at Owatonna," recalls Reds captain David Youngblood, who admits that he himself was "not nearly as dedicated to victory at all cost as my fellow captains."[157] Swanson went on to be an outstanding athlete at UMass, and then played professional football for the Boston Patriots (1967-68) and Cincinnati Bengals (1969).

Cabin inspection, which had been a fixture since the Ropioa days, was another opportunity for recognition. Each summer, one cabin from both the Senior and Junior divisions was named Inspection Winner for accumulating the most points through daily clean up and inspection of their living quarters. Individual campers were also recognized for receiving the most "personals" by keeping their personal bunks and trunks tidy. The Inspection winners in 1957 were Cabin 7 in the Senior division and Cabin 13 in the Junior division; the Personal winners were Flip Steckler in the Senior division, and Ira Bartelstone and Fred Martin in the Junior division. At the end of the summer, winners were driven into Naples for a steak dinner at Howard Johnson's and a movie in Bridgton.[158]

The plaques also show the first recorded awarding of the White Feather in 1957—its counterpart, the Black Feather, would not be created until a couple years later. Edwards created the award, and it was comparable to the "R" award from the Ropioa days.[159] As described in the *Echo* newsletter:

> The white feather here at camp has a deep significance for it means that the camper has done an outstanding piece of work here. He has been an all-around good camper. As the camper adds years to his Owatonna summers he will have the opportunity to add white feathers to his headdress.[160]

Feather recipients were apparently selected in a meeting that included both older campers and counselors, a process that would eventually change to just include counselors. Criteria for receiving the award was laid out in the *Echo*. Courage and bravery were requisite but also the following qualities:

- Attitude toward and application of Christian Science
- Unselfishness, consideration and thoughtfulness
- Self-discipline, does he make demands on himself?
- Clean thinking, no rumor monger, foul language or off color stories
- Spirit and team loyalty, working together for common good
- Humility
- Good camper[161]

The first White Feather winners were C.I.T.s Sterling Hamilton and David Youngblood, and Junior division campers Jeff Hamlin and Jeff Kelly, although 11 others were also nominated. The feathers were handed out at the final Council Fire of the summer, which took place on a Sunday night and was attended by parents.[162] Youngblood remembers it was a solemn ceremony that featured Head Counselor Ty Anderson dressed up in costume:

> We had to stand in a circle and Ty walked around to select the honorees. I didn't think I had a chance after the extravagant qualifications were listed at morning meeting, but somehow, as he passed me, Ty slammed me on the shoulder, I stumbled back several steps, then followed him to the head of the fire, where a few other senior campers and I were honored. It was a very big deal, and I still remember the tingle of having that feather put on.[163]

Council Fire itself bore resemblance to the P.G.T. meetings of Ropioa, but it included new elements that would remain for decades. The meeting was presided over by Chief White Eagle. Games were led by Warrior Black Raven, and the three teams competed against each other in tests of agility and strength, as well as in song. Campers could challenge each other individually, and winners received a verbal "heep-how." Awards were given to campers for achievements from the week. Finally, the meeting concluded with the singing of "By the Blazing Council Fire's Light," and then the listening of Taps. As described in the *Echo*, campers joined hands "as a token of the close bond of brotherhood, the underlying principle of all camp life."[164]

As for camp life in 1957, a picture of it is captured in the *Echo's* description of Backwards Day, a fun tradition in which the daily routine and roles were reversed. Campers became counselors, with C.I.T. David Youngblood taking over for Edwards as Director. As indicated from this schedule—although in the reverse—it is apparent that Owatonna today has hardly changed since Edwards's day.

7:30am	Taps by counselor Jim Day's trombone
8:00am	A hike backwards to the Birches, then Supper with uniforms on backwards
8:30am	Flag lowering
8:45am	Camper-counselor baseball
11:00am	Rest Hour
12:30pm	Lunch (dessert first)
1:15pm	Third activity period
2:15pm	Second activity period
3:15pm	First activity period
4:15pm	Church meeting (hymns sung backwards)

4:30pm	Quiet Hour
4:45pm	Cabin cleanup
6:00pm	Breakfast
6:30pm	Flag raising
9:00pm	Calisthenics
9:01pm	Reveille[165]

Activities in 1957 included all the usual ones, as well as photography. In fact, for many years there was a photography dark room attached to the Old Lighthouse.[166] Boxing and wrestling were also available. A Junior Life Saving program was part of the waterfront curriculum. There were inter-camp matches, too, such as a baseball win against O-AT-KA in August. Like always, joint activities with Newfound included Sunday School, a Christian Science lecture, talent shows, and dances. For trips, campers went fishing on the Saco River, hiked up Bald Pate, and stayed overnight in the AMC hut (Lake of the Clouds) on Mt. Washington. Edwards hinted in a letter to parents that the next year campers would possibly tackle Mt. Katahdin, the highest mountain in Maine at 5,269 feet.[167]

Owatonna was growing, too. The staff increased from about a dozen counselors in 1956 to 17 in 1957.[168] For campers, enrollment doubled from the previous summer, numbering 73 campers, with more than two-thirds coming from the Tri-State area. Winthrop True had traveled the furthest, the only camper to have come from St. Louis. There were five C.I.T.s and three Junior Counselors, although it is not clear exactly what these programs entailed at this point.[169] One clue comes from a letter written by a parent to Trustee Frank Connor a few months after the end of the 1957 summer. In it, Howard Galloway, whose son John was a camper, suggests that Owatonna implement a "work program" for older boys. In exchange for a reduced tuition, these boys could wait on tables during meals and keep buildings and walking trails clean. If they weren't already, these ideas would soon enough become elements of Owatonna's C.I.T. program.[170]

Additionally, it was likely under Edwards that the concept of the "Owatonna Man" originated. An early reference to it is seen in an "editorial" in the *Echo,* contrasting the camping man with the "city softie." The latter clung to his milkshakes, TV, and comic books, but would probably

> never know the deep satisfaction of roughing it on a wilderness trip; of getting up with the sun and exercising vigorously in the clear, crisp air; of eating a man-sized breakfast to hold him through a morning packed with activities demanding concentration, persistence, and agility. The cabin overnight, the satisfaction of getting close to nature and learning to fend for himself against the elements, the drive for team spirit and unity and the close association resulting from it, the mystery of Indian ritual in the Council Ring, the glow, both universal and outward of hard physical activity and achieving a difficult goal—these are the rewards that escape the city dweller—these are the measure of a camping man—an Owatonna man.[171]

In their own words, the campers showed that they had taken this concept to heart. Asked what they had gained from the 1957 season, Ricky Pilsbury was succinct: "Love my neighbor as myself." Pete Wilson was more descriptive: "I think I have gained leadership in helping the captain of my team, responsibility in helping with the cabin, and I have definitely gained from Christian Science. I've had quite a few healings. Camp has helped me in my sports. I've gained a girl." Peter

Vernon was honest: "I have gained 9 ½ pounds over this wonderful summer at Camp Owatonna."[172]

In 1958, Edwards's second summer as Director, elements of Owatonna programming continued to take shape. Ty Anderson was back as Head Counselor, overseeing 76 campers and 17 counselors. Bill Bodine, who seems to have been acting informally as Edwards's Assistant Director, reported that in 1958 they implemented a new plan for activity periods that separated the Junior and Senior campers, suggesting that before the change, campers of all ages participated in activities together. Edwards thought the new system might better allow younger campers to develop necessary beginner skills through age-appropriate programming.[173]

As for the activities, the addition of new sailing Tech Dinghies were a hit with the campers, and they allowed Owatonna to compete in a sailing regatta against 18 other camps.[174] Waterfront counselor Nat Frothingham accomplished something "new in the annals of Owatonna" by making a big activity of canoeing![175] Outside of Camp, new hiking excursions tackled Mt. Chocorua and Mt. Katahdin, as promised.[176] There was also now the opportunity to take a trip to Boston, which continues to be an offering today, typically geared towards those who have never visited before. Campers toured The Mother Church, the Christian Science Publishing Society, and Mary Baker Eddy's historic house.[177]

Further developments included the creation of standardized administrative lists and forms for counselors to use, such as inspection and team scoring sheets.[178] Bill Bodine and Ty Anderson were responsible for inspecting the thirteen cabins, using a scoring template that is little unchanged decades later (see Appendix).

The team scoring sheet shows how weekly points were tallied for individual campers and teams.[179] Campers who earned more than 300 points in a season were awarded team feathers.[180] The competitive point system was found to be an effective motivator, turning even mundane tasks into opportunities to display excellence. For example, Edwards reported to parents that a "noteworthy development" was campers' positive response to team cleanup projects on Saturday mornings.[181]

On Saturday afternoons, the teams competed in sports: "The Reds gained on their rivals by a fine showing in the ribbon track meet held Saturday before a host of visitors," reported a 1958 issue of the *Echo*.[182] One new challenge Edwards invented in 1957 was the Hill Run, an uphill run from the edge of the Owatonna Beach up to the Lighthouse.[183] He explained decades later:

> One tradition that was truly a God-send was the way we overcame the griping that all campers indulged in when they had to trudge up the beach trail to the camp proper for lunch—a distance of about 400 yards up a winding trail obstructed by huge jutting rocks. Doc Singer, our waterfront man, and I were keenly aware of how much the lads treasured team points awarded them for certain individual exploits. So, we began to run a race for each camper who wanted to convert a good time into team points. Doc had a starting pistol at the bottom, and I had a stopwatch at the top. This devilish device produced miracles! First, it introduced competition and team pride; second, it did away with the griping; and third, it began to produce better shape in the boys' physical condition, and eventually, after successive years, stars in track and field

with championship times in 444, 880, and mile runs at their own high school meets—incredible![184]

On Saturday evenings, the teams met in Council Fire, which continued to evolve in these early years. The lighting of the fire, for example, became an opportunity for creativity, often masterminded by campcraft counselor Art Scholet. At the third Council Fire, two campers did a "heel and toe dance imploring the Great Spirit for the magical gift of fire."[185] At the final Council Fire (and in front of parents) a flaming arrow was used![186] Elements of the meeting included counselors telling Native American-inspired tales and the presence of the "Great Chief." There were also nature reports, such as "one account of a battle with a raccoon" by Junior division Blues Pete Kinney and Kim Cuniberti.[187] New décor appeared with the addition of Year Rocks, lining the path to the council ring. These could be painted in team colors by campers who had attended a full three summers or five summers; the highly coveted 10-year rock was painted in white.

Capping off the 1958 summer was the annual banquet, a tradition since Ropioa times, although now it featured the very important announcement of which team earned the most points that summer. Before the big reveal, there was a feast of chicken, corn on the cob, hot rolls, green beans, and ice cream sundaes. There were speeches from Phil Edwards and Trustee Frank Connor, followed by cake and various camper awards. Finally, the team captains—the Blues' Peter Vernon, the Reds' Don Gibbs, and the Greens' Steve Ross (who was standing in for captain Gene Morrison)—stepped forward to receive their team plaques; the Greens won with 6,451 points, then came the Blues with 6,229 points and the Reds with 5,409 points.

A delicious cake baked by Pearl Baker was a highlight of the night.[188] Pearl and her husband Ervin were a local couple who would work at Camp for the next three decades. Erv was the facilities manager, and Pearl was Owatonna's excellent baker (during the year she was a cook at Bridgton Academy). Although they were not Christian Scientists, interestingly they were allowed to enroll their son Perry as a camper. The Bakers were beloved by generations of Owatonnans, Pearl for her baked goods and Erv for his Maine humor.

Edwards remained Director for five more summers through 1963, and there were a number of notable developments during these years. An important one was the establishment of the Black Feather award in 1959. Its original qualification was straightforward: "given to outstanding athletes who also demonstrate sportsmanlike attitude."[189] The first Black Feather winners were Senior division camper Bart Jealous—excellent in baseball, tennis, boxing, basketball, football, and judo—and Junior camper Buz Brewster—excellent in baseball, basketball, swimming, riflery, boxing, tennis, and waterskiing.[190]

Together, the White and Black Feathers became the symbols of excellence at Owatonna, although not without some questioning their impact on the campers. At a Trustee meeting in August 1960, "there was much feeling regarding the advisability of the present system of awarding the white feather and the emotional strain it causes." Therefore, the Trustees decided to award feathers at a secret campfire rather than at the more public Parents Weekend, and to only recognize recipients, not also nominees.[191]

Also in 1960, a new activity period structure was introduced, based on visits to other camps in the area. The blocks were as follows:

- Beach Period, including waterskiing
- Field Period, including track and riflery
- Activity Period, including campcraft, arts & crafts, dramatics, nature
- Field Period, including tennis, basketball, baseball, etc.[192]

Activities were separated by age divisions, which changed in 1962 from two divisions—Juniors and Seniors—to four divisions—Scouts, Braves, Warriors, and Chiefs.[193]

Improvements were made in all activity areas. Down at the Beach, the Big Float was upgraded to include a slide and diving tower in 1957.[194] Head of the Waterfront Ray "Doc" B. Singer requested they extend the docks to build a crib area and water polo pool for the 1962 season.[195] Doc seems to have been a slightly older but influential member of the staff during this era. He had been a Head Counselor at Camp Leelanau and taught swimming for over 20 years at Cleveland High School in St. Louis. "He is one crackerjack of a swimming instructor," wrote Edwards.[196] Doc joined the Owatonna staff in 1959, and his wife Dorothy became the camp practitioner over at the Birches. He ended up buying a retirement home nearby and worked with Head of Facilities Ervin Baker until passing away in 1966.[197]

A big addition to Owatonna came in 1961 with the purchase of Cherry Island.[198] The island had originally been part of the Joseph Chaplin property that became Ropioa, but it was sold in 1911 to a neighbor, Charles E. Roberts. During the Ropioa years, it was known as Raspberry Island, a destination for canoeing and fishing. It's unknown when or why the name changed, but it was called Cherry Island by 1958, purchased in 1961 from Leona Roberts, and fully conveyed by 1963.[199] The quarter mile out-and-back distance became a core part of the Owatonna swim test.

1959 Owatonna trustees and their wives at the Waldorf Astoria with Gordon MacRae (center). Phoebe F. Connor, Boyd Jones, Lydia Cooper, Pat Stevens, MacRae, Sally Romero, Al Romero, Bill Stevens, and Frank Hayden Connor.

Also on the waterfront, Camp was blessed with a generous gift when Hollywood movie star Gordon MacRae donated a brand-new Magnolia motorboat in August 1959. MacRae had been a Ropioa camper in the 1930s and a favorite camper of Al Romero, who was now on the Owatonna Board of Trustees. Romero remembers the two of them rising early to go fishing down on Long Lake, and then bringing their catch back to be fried by the cook for breakfast. A memorable cabin skit involved Romero and MacRae acting out "Cinderella," with little MacRae as the Prince and Romero as a 6'1"-tall Cinderella—no doubt it was a sight to see![200] As an adult, MacRae became a successful film and Broadway actor, but he never forgot his love for Ropioa. The new boat was a hit with the campers as it was powerful enough to pull two skiers at the same time.[201]

At camp proper, there were improvements, too. In 1957, the Rec Hall was fixed up and the Lodge was painted.[202] A basketball court was laid down by the east entrance, where it remains today, and in 1961 a barbecue cook-out pit was built by the Lodge.[203] A fourteenth cabin was added, and all cabins were screened in.[204] The addition of an athletics field was another significant addition. Edwards explained decades later:

> Between the cabins and the rec hall ran a long widespread ditch running toward the end of a field. I asked the Board for approval to hire a bulldozer operator to level a huge plot of ground, giving us a huge soccer-football field encircled by a running track. Beyond that lay the baseball field. This project enabled us to move into active inter-team competition plus many after dinner team competitions (such as "Run sheepie run" and "Capture the Flag" contests).[205]

Healthy competition naturally became a signature part of Owatonna's culture. The many athletic challenges were meant to provide opportunities for campers to grow and shine. Old record books document some of the athletic feats of the era.[206] The Senior division record for the Hill Run in 1961 was set by that year's Reds team captain John Lyon, who ran an impressive time of 1:15—just one second shy of counselor Rich Overby's record of 1:14 set in 1957. During a Junior division baseball game against Camp Wingo in 1963, future Greens team captain Andy Rodgers threw a no hitter. Buz Brewster was unstoppable on the basketball court in 1962—he scored 34 points against Camp Zakelo on Thursday, and then he put up 40 points against Camp Wingo on Friday. Owatonna counselors got to have their fun too—against a Ranger Lodge basketball team in 1963, Pete

Stackhouse scored 36 points, and Ty Anderson just edged him out with 39 points.

Edwards continued to think of new activities for the campers, not always with success. His idea for amateur flying lessons didn't make it past the Board of Trustees in 1961. On the other hand, amateur radio was introduced in 1963 by counselors Don Leigh Koch, Bruce Dale, and Jim Chapman—Edwards even offered his skills as a former Naval communicator.[207]

One longtime activity, horseback riding, was cut, however. It had been a feature of both the boys' and girls' camps dating back to Ropioa. Since the 1940s, campers had taken lessons from Steve Burns, who lived in the farmhouse near the entrance to Ropioa—a riding ring was located where Owatonna's tennis courts reside today, and the stables were just south by the barbecue pit.[208] When Burns retired in 1961, the Trustees had to reconsider the future of the program. For a time, campers rode offsite at the "Hacienda" in Fryeburg, but eventually the program became too expensive and was discontinued.[209]

After being promoted in 1963 to Assistant Headmaster at Principia Upper School, Phil Edwards stepped down as Director.[210] Over his seven years, he implemented many of the traditions that still define Owatonna today. His work continued when he later served on the Owatonna Board of Trustees throughout the 1960s and 1970s.[211] In the following years, he continued to teach and coach at Principia with much success, winning two Missouri state tennis titles and two sectional titles. Always an athlete, Edwards played tennis competitively in adult leagues and won several U.S. Tennis Association championships. He was named to the USTA Hall of Fame in 1996 and to the Principia Athletics Hall of Fame in 2010.[212]

Early 1960s Tech Dinghies

Early 1960s Arts and Crafts

Late 1950s Gordie Jones, Pete Stackhouse, Fred Martin, Don Steckler, Tim Bayless

Late 1950s Pete Van Dyck and Glenn Johnson

Early 1960s Catching air at the trampoline pit

Early 1960s Fun at the Beach

Early 1960s Phil Edwards inspecting

Early 1960s Off to Sunday School

1960s All-camp photo

ca. 1966 Louise and Ty Anderson

THE ANDERSON YEARS
(1964-66)

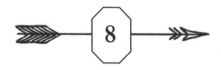

Stepping into the Director position was Thiers "Ty" Anderson. Like Edwards, Anderson had been an outstanding Principia athlete in baseball, football, and basketball. At the Principia Upper School, his football team set a school record for the longest streak of winning seasons, unbroken for 24 years. At Principia College, his football team had an undefeated season in 1954.[213] Like others, Anderson had come to Owatonna by way of Camp Passaconaway, and he was part of the staff for Owatonna's first season in 1956, during which he oversaw team sports. He was Edwards's Head Counselor in 1957 and '58, then went away to serve four years in the U.S. Navy. After his service, he became a coach at the Upper School and returned to Owatonna as Head Counselor for Edwards's last summer in 1963. Although Anderson was not yet 30 years old, with his background in education and sports, as well as his time with Owatonna since its beginning, he was a natural choice to lead Camp.

Anderson was Director for three summers from 1964 through 1966. A snapshot of this era is captured in the staff handbook prepared by counselors Donald Bliss and Nolen

Harter.[214] The four-period activity area system implemented by Phil Edwards in 1960 had been refined into the periods that remain today: Swimming, Boat Dock, Sports, Individuals. Cabin Nights were on Thursdays, and Activity Clubs were on Sunday evenings, with diverse offerings such as golf, fishing, photography, and producing the *Echo* newsletter. The chorus club prepared its members for talent shows, of course, but also for "serenading Newfound by canoe."

Mealtime was perhaps a bit more formal than today. Campers received weekly table assignments each Sunday noon (which lasted at least into the late 1990s). C.I.T.s were held to a high standard as waiters. Their performance was rated each week by counselors, and these ratings were used to evaluate them for future counselor positions. Terry Batty was a C.I.T. in 1960 and remembers waiting on meals three times a day—he was happy to report that he never dropped a tray that summer.[215] Despite the formalities, meals were also opportunities for "enthusiastic counselors" to generate camp spirit. The staff handbook advised:

> Spontaneous talk in unison among the tables is to be encouraged. For example, when a counselor has an elbow on the table, another table chants, "Jack Smith strong and able, get your elbow off the table." Other more creative forms of group teasing are welcome if in good taste. Even more welcome is the spontaneous singing of songs from the camp sheets.[216]

The Tripping program expanded in these years with new offerings, such as to Acadia, Flagstaff-Bigelow, Ogunquit Beach, and even a gold-panning expedition. An extended 10-day trip down the Allagash river in 1965 was memorable not only for the excessive rain and bugs, but also because Curt Bowersock tried to put his pants on while speeding down the rapids, of course causing him to fall overboard.[217]

New traditions appeared at this time, too, such as Owatonna Yacht Club dances with the Newfound girls, the Boat Tug of War, and the annual Newfound-Owatonna Water Carnival.[218] Established traditions continued to evolve, as well. For instance, at the final banquet, teams now created table centerpieces, and team plaques were brought in by former team members.[219] At Council Fire, the Grand Shaman began leaving a word-of-the-week at the close of each meeting—the last word of the 1966 season was *humility*.[220] Counselors were no longer referred to as Woodcrafter but as *Sachem*, an Algonquin word for a chief.[221] The criteria for the White and Black Feathers was further simplified:

White	**Black**
▪ Contributions to cabin	▪ Athletic ability
▪ Contributions to activities	▪ Humility
▪ Contributions to trips	▪ Versatility
▪ Contributions to teams	▪ Sportsmanship[222]

The *Echo* also documented in detail a Feather Fire, which reveals the introduction of new characters—the Four Winds—and shows an order of events that would remain unchanged for decades: All the campers first turned away from the fire; the Winds then brought winners to the center of the ring before carrying them away into the woods; when called, the campers were then carried back and set before the Grand Shaman, who bestowed them their feather awards.[223]

Organizationally, Owatonna grew to its largest enrollment yet with over 100 campers and 30 staff members in both 1965 and '66.²²⁴ Interestingly, a large contingent of campers in the 1960s came from the Christian Science Sunday School in Ardmore, Pennsylvania, located on the main line of the Pennsylvania Railroad, just outside of Philadelphia. Scott Moeller says they referred to themselves as the "A-C-ers", for the Ardmore Church.²²⁵

In 1965, Owatonna completed its payments to Benjamin DeMascola, meaning that it fully owned the property. Also that year, longtime Newfound Director and owner Dorothy "Becky" Horton Cobb retired, selling the girls' camp to the Owatonna Board of Trustees.²²⁶ Newfound and Owatonna continued to operate as individual not-for-profit organizations and would not become a single corporation until the 1980s.²²⁷

The summer of 1965 also marked Owatonna's 10-year anniversary. Anderson summarized some of the changes that had taken place in that first decade in an *Echo* article: the Beach was enlarged, docks added, and Cherry Island acquired; the Boat House was rebuilt; basketball moved up the hill; a volleyball court replaced the horse-riding ring. Some aspects hadn't changed: the Hill Run was still a popular challenge; Pearl Baker's great cooking and one-of-a-kind cinnamon buns continued; and Christian Science was still at the heart of Owatonna's daily life.²²⁸

The anniversary was celebrated at the 1965 end-of-summer banquet, which was attended by special guests, including former Directors Tom Hilton and Phil Edwards, former Waterfront head Doc Singer, and Trustees John Cooper and Frank Connor.²²⁹ Counselor John Leopold penned an article for the *Echo* reflecting on what Camp had meant to him. Leopold had been at Owatonna every summer since its founding and so was tasked with recording its early history. He concluded that Camp was special because it was a "proving ground" like no other. "It is my sincere hope," he wrote, "that the boys who come to Owatonna for decades to come will find this unique feature of the camp and keep it close to them for the rest of their lives."[230]

Anderson stepped down after the 1966 season but later served on the Owatonna Board of Trustees throughout the 1970s.[231] He continued his career at Principia, where he coached record-setting football teams in 1966 and '68. He himself would be named to the Principia Athletics Hall of Fame in 2014.[232] After his time at Principia, Anderson moved to Texas and had a two-decade career in finance. Before he left Owatonna, however, he named Fred Beyer as his successor.[233]

ca. 1966 Canoeing activity period

ca. 1966 Clark Johnson at bat, counselors Pete Stackhouse and John Leopold on the bench ca. 1966 Playing hoops

ca. 1966 Counselor Alec Jones rappelling

ca. 1966 Looking for scenic views

ca. 1966 Swim lessons

ca. 1966 Lining up for lunch

ca. 1966 Counselor Pete Stackhouse

1966 Terry Batty (center) with his C.I.T.s, including Bruce Cameron, Gary Heard, Tom Neale, Dana Wilson, and Chip Miller

1967 Fred and Phyllis Beyer

1968 Verne Ullom

THE BEYER & ULLOM
YEARS (1967-68)

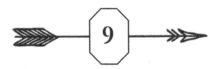

Fred Beyer was a burly-looking guy, according to Jamie Bollinger, who was a first-year Scout at the time.²³⁴ Bollinger remembers Beyer pumping out push-ups and pull-ups in front of the entire camp, which checks out given that Beyer was a former Christian Science Chaplain in the U.S. Army. He had served 14 years on both active duty and in the reserves, achieving the rank of Major. Although a non-combatant, Beyer had received a Bronze Star for meritorious service in the Korean War. Once in the reserves, he worked for many years as a Christian Science Minister to cadets at West Point, probably until 1964 when he left military service.²³⁵

By 1967, Beyer had become the Dean of Boys at the Daycroft School, a school for Christian Scientists in Greenwich, Connecticut.²³⁶ This schedule allowed him to also become Director of Owatonna that summer, and of course he brought his four boys along. Three decades later, his son Eric reflected on that summer, writing:

> I was about 12 years old and my father was chosen to be Owatonna's next Director (1966-1967). So my brothers and

parents were there for the summer too. My father is one of those adults who maintained the ability to play and think like a kid and probably enjoyed Camp as much as any camper. He and the staff built the first rope swing, built a 130-foot slide down into the lake, got a rock-climbing program started, and had fun. We all did.[237]

Other fun additions include a rope for rappelling, installed off the tall elm trees by the Birches, as well as a tightrope wire behind the Braves cabins.[238] The rope swing and waterslide were constructed by counselors Arthur Dean and Nolen Harter, who remembers the waterslide was a hit with campers but that it was also short-lived.

The slide was built with a wooden frame and lined with plastic tarp; water was pumped from the lake up to the top of the slide.[239] When Trustee Frank Connor was visiting, he wanted to try it out himself. There were strict rules about keeping your hands in your lap, but Connor still managed to encounter some stray branches on his way down. So, the waterslide was retired shortly thereafter. Or as Jamie Bollinger put it, instead of removing the tree, they removed the slide.[240]

The rope swing, however, still exists to this day, although not in its original form or location. The structure that Harter and Dean built was between the Boat Dock and the Owatonna Beach. It was also a bit larger back then. Eric Beyer remembers watching counselor Bill Stitt go off the rope swing wearing water skis and flying across Long Lake.[241] The swing was later downsized and rebuilt in the mid-1980s by facilities man Paul Field where it now stands near Newfound.[242]

Nolen Harter, the swing's original builder, had been recruited in 1962 by Phil Edwards to teach waterskiing, and he'd

1967 The original rope swing

been coming back ever since. Professionally, he was a teacher, having taught at the Daycroft School and now more locally at Oxford Hills High School in South Paris, Maine. As a "science guy" he came up with creative new ways to light the fire during Council Fire, and stories about this abound from these years. Once, he used a liquid chemical to mysteriously set the wood alight on its own; for the mid-season beach Council Fire, he sent a flare into the fire along a wire that ran all the way from Cherry

Island; he even constructed a catapult that could launch flaming toilet paper rolls, but the contraption never made it past the testing phase.[243]

Another construction built by Harter and Arthur Dean that is still in use every day at Camp is the Head Table in the Lodge.[244] Although he wasn't on staff during the summer of 1968, he and Dean built and delivered the round dining table with a Lazy Susan turntable in the center. The new table was apparently needed because the original one had been damaged. As the story goes, a certain Black Feather winner (who was an otherwise excellent athlete) bet his Red teammates (who had just finished setting up the Lodge for Saturday lunch) that he could jump over the Head Table. He didn't make it.[245]

After Beyer moved on, Verne Ullom became Director for the 1968 summer. Ullom had worked at Camp for several seasons, including at least two years as an Assistant Director to Phil Edwards.[246] Like his predecessors, he was an accomplished athlete; he had been a football star at the University of Cincinnati, and he had played one season in the National Football League in 1944 for the no-longer-extant Brooklyn Tigers.[247] Since then, he had coached at Bates College in Maine, Principia College, and Colby College.[248]

A snapshot of the 1968 summer is seen in Ullom's planning documents, which include a breakdown of the activity offerings that year:[249]

Waterfront	Crafts	Individual	Athletics
Swim	Arts	Gymnastics	Baseball
Sailing	Camp	Riflery	Basketball
Canoeing	Campfire	Archery	Soccer
Rowing	Trips	Tennis	Football
Waterski	Music	Badminton	Track
			Volleyball
			Newcombe

Ullom was only Director for one summer, but he oversaw one significant change by adding a fourth team: the Ogallala Golds. The need for an extra team may have been due to a larger enrollment of campers, and it was also much more conducive to intra-camp competition—with only three teams, there had always been one team sitting out on the sidelines. Although team assignments were meant to be permanent, to facilitate the formation of the Golds, some campers were pulled from other teams. The first captain of the Golds was C.I.T. Pete Wagner from Guilford, Connecticut, who led them in their debut summer to a 1st-place finish.

The Golds took their name from the Oglala tribe, one of the seven bands of the Lakota Sioux, located in modern South Dakota. Many elements of the stereotypical Native American are drawn from Lakota culture, such as teepees, feathered war bonnets, and galloping horse-riders. Famous Lakota leaders include Crazy Horse, Sitting Bull, and Red Cloud. In Sioux, *oglala* means "they who scatter their own."[250] They were nomadic buffalo hunters who migrated to the plains during the 18th century and resisted American expansionism for 40 years during the 19th century. Today, the Lakota continue to be one of the largest Native American tribes. In 1980, they were offered $105 million from the U.S. government for the earlier seizure of their lands, but the Lakota refused the payment. Instead, they continue to demand full sovereignty over their former lands.[251]

In early 1969, Verne Ullom resigned as Director in order to pursue more coaching opportunities. Before he left, he suggested to Frank Connor that waterski counselor John Bower be considered for the position. After the Board of Trustees extended the offer to Bower, Ullom and his wife Doris helped prepare Bower and his wife Bonnie for the role.[252]

1966 Nolen Harter, Scott Beyer, and Fred Beyer

1967 Tightrope walking behind the Braves cabins

1967 Hanging out

ca. 1966 Ready for adventure

1970s John and Bonnie Bower

THE BOWER YEARS
(1969-75)

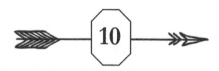

John Bower was Director for the next seven summers from 1969 through 1975—one of the longest continuous runs in the role. Bower is also one of the most accomplished athletes to be affiliated with Owatonna.[253] Born in Auburn, Maine, he was already a two-time Olympian when he took the job in his late 20s. Nordic skiing was his sport—he had won four state titles in high school, an NCAA Championship at Middlebury College, competed in the 1962 World Championships, and the 1964 and '68 Olympics. A few months before he was on Owatonna's staff in the summer of 1968, Bower shocked the skiing world by becoming the first American to win the King's Cup at the Holmenkollen Ski Festival in Norway.

In 1969, Bower retired from competitive skiing and became the coach of Middlebury's ski team. His coaching schedule and location in Vermont allowed him to run Owatonna during the summers. His wife, Bonnie, who was a former Newfound counselor, as well as the coach of the women's ski team at Middlebury, became the Business Manager for both camps during this time.[254]

Bower's love for Christian Science and athletics made him a good fit for Owatonna. As a child, he had been healed of asthma, and so using Christian Science became an integral part of his successes later in life, including in his famous win at Holmenkollen. He wrote about several of these experiences for the Christian Science periodicals.[255] Chic Johnson, a camper at the time, remembers, "My recollection of John was that he knew how to apply Christian Science to athletics. He could articulate things that were helpful to athletes.... He was a real student of Christian Science."[256]

Bower also expected a high level of discipline from his campers. Gary Crandell was the Assistant Director in 1969 and chuckled as he explained to me that a "Bower Shower" involved dumping cold water on campers or counselors who slept through reveille.[257] After lights out one night in 1974, Bower went to investigate why so much noise was coming from the Chiefs in Cabin 1. When one camper's cheeky reply to Bower caused his cabinmates to crack up in even more laughter, they quickly all found themselves doing push-ups in their underwear as mosquito bait on the front porch![258]

One noteworthy change marked the beginning of Bower's tenure in 1969. Up to this point, Camp had always been an eight-week-long program, with most campers staying the full session. At the close of the previous summer, however, the Board of Trustees announced a switch to a seven-week program.[259] The explanation was that many American schools had begun starting earlier in September and ending later in June, so Camp's schedule had to adjust accordingly.

A few memories from 1969 indicate that pranks had become an Owatonna specialty. A Newfound newsletter recounts how raiders from Owatonna ambushed a Sunday Song

Service with water balloons, kidnapping five maidens. A Newfound ransom of marshmallows was subsequently delivered in exchange for the hostages.[260]

Yet, co-ed relations were not always so "hostile." The girls of Gaiety Gables had a tradition of presenting Owatonna with a gift every summer. At the mid-season Council Fire in 1969, they presented their Owatonna brethren with a handmade drum, painted green, white, and black.[261] There were also special co-ed events, such as Scottish Day, which featured Scottish-inspired activities and culminated in a Scottish sword dance performed by the Scouts of Cabin 14: Jamie Bollinger, Jamie MacKenzie, Rich Coomber, and (big) Al Boyd.[262]

Other performances had higher stakes. On Store Nights at Owatonna, each table at dinner would give some kind of entertaining presentation that was judged by the Head Table. First place would get first dibs on goodies from the Camp Store. Rich Coomber's go-to candies were the root beer barrels and fireballs; if you were "in the know," says Scott Moeller, you could ask for your Snickers or Mars bar from the freezer rather than at room temperature, which was often half melted.[263]

While team competition remained much the same in these years, there were finally some changes in terms of who was winning. Since Owatonna had started in 1957, the Blues had generally been the dominant team out of the three. In fact, the first two Triple Crown Winners had been Blues—Terry Rodgers in 1962 and Glenn Johnson in '65; the Triple Crown is an unofficial achievement (and a term coined decades later) for captains who not only lead their team to a 1st-place finish, but also win both the White and Black Feathers.[264] According to Phil Edwards, early on "somehow the Blues got the Yankee complex and seemed to emerge champions although it was always a last-ditch struggle."²⁶⁵ So far, the Blues had finished in 1st place eight of the first 12 summers.

However, starting in 1969, it was the Reds who began a period of dominance. They had won before—Edwards remembers the banquet in 1960 when "the Shawsheen Reds actually won, all heck broke loose!"²⁶⁶ During John Bower's seven years, however, the Reds took 1st place four times. With athletes like runner Jamie Bollinger—who set a Hill Run record of 1:09—and Jeff Wayman and Burke Miller—Triple Crown Winners in 1971 and '74—it was a golden era for the Reds.

The Blues, on the other hand, fell to last place for the first time, if only briefly, in 1972. Erik Olsen was a C.I.T. for the Blues that year—in fact, he was the only C.I.T. on the team. Unusually, his younger brother Peter had already been initiated into a different team. But Erik recalls John Bower pulling him aside and asking if he would consider joining the Blues, who were seriously shorthanded on Senior division campers. As the only C.I.T., Erik was elected team captain more or less by default. The Blues came in 4th that year, and they wouldn't win another 1st place until 1980.²⁶⁷

There were a couple of other "firsts" during Bower's years. In 1972, the Trustees hired the first Executive Director, Robert Wilson, who oversaw both Newfound and Owatonna.²⁶⁸ A new Counselor Cabin was built in 1973 because the original one had burned down after a lightning strike in 1972.²⁶⁹ In 1973, Bower also introduced a new special trips program, advertised as the Pack 'N Paddle program. It allowed campers to make offsite camping trips the primary focus of their summers, and it lasted for a few years.²⁷⁰

The trips program at this time was "pretty rustic," remembers Chic Johnson. There were no tents back then, so if it rained at night, you simply put a poncho over your sleeping bag. As a Chief in 1970, Johnson went on a memorable Allagash canoeing trip with several C.I.T.s, including his brother Glenn, as well as Peter Martin and Duncan Martin. Chic still remembers Peter and Duncan—who shared a last name but were not related—flipping their canoe on the way down Chase Rapids. While everyone else sailed through the rapids without incident, Chic and Glenn's canoe was weighed down by the group's very large wooden box of food, which seemed to pull them into every rock all the way down.[271]

1970 Members of the Allagash canoeing trip

A fixture of Owatonna camping trips throughout the 1970s—and likely for years before and after—was an old Chevy pick-up truck affectionately named the Green Monster. It had been customized with a home-built wooden canopy in the back, and it was often used to transport campers up and down the Newfound Hill, as well as all over Maine and New Hampshire for various camping trips. The canopy was eventually covered in a dark canvas tarp, so when campers loaded up for a trip, they'd sit in darkness getting jostled to and fro, listening to the superstructure creak and groan while trying to keep their pancake breakfast down.

A couple changes closed out Bower's final years as Director. One was the discontinuation of the riflery program. It was one of the more popular activities, and Owatonna had demonstrated some prowess by finishing sixth in the 1964 National Postals tournament, ahead of many military schools. A "world famous" gunsmith named Eugene Clarence "Bob" Horton maintained the camp rifles in the off-season, and some campers were able to spend memorable afternoons visiting his shop, Horton Ballistics, in the backwoods of Waterford, Maine.[272] Despite these strengths, the future of the riflery program was discussed at a Trustee meeting in September 1968—the meeting notes indicating that they would look for direction from the American Camp Association, which was expected to release a recommendation on the topic.[273] Owatonna continued to offer it at least through the 1973 season, but it seems to fade from the historical record after that.[274]

A new activity that appeared in the Bower years, however, was fencing. Englishman Tony Coomber, a teacher and fencing coach from New Jersey, brought the sport to camp, and an old

ca. 1972 Fencing lessons with Tony Coomber

fenced-in tennis court adjacent to the archery range was repurposed for several years as the fencing arena.[275]

Finally, in Bower's last summer of 1975, Newfound and Owatonna became a member of the American Camp Association (ACA). The ACA was originally established in 1910. Starting in 1948, it began offering a voluntary accreditation process, which measures levels of proficiency and safety against nationally recognized standards.[276] In the early 1970s, less than a third of the 11,000 camps in the United States were members of the ACA, but the push for greater regulation and oversight was growing. Ultimately, national standards were meant to protect campers from lax safety adherents and protect camps from lawsuits.[277]

Bower stepped down from his positions at Owatonna and Middlebury in order to become the Nordic skiing program director for the U.S. Ski Team from 1975 to 1980.[278] He then became the Athletic Director at Principia College before returning again to the U.S. Ski Team coaching staff. Bower had been a member of the National Ski Hall of Fame in 1969, was ranked as one of Maine's greatest athletes by *Sports Illustrated* in 1999, and was named to the Middlebury College Hall of Fame in 2014.[279]

John and Bonnie continued to be involved with Newfound and Owatonna for many years. They became the first Directors of Family Camp, and Bonnie would later serve as Executive Director in the 1980s, as well as in other roles in the 1990s and 2000s.[280]

2011 In later years, John Bower towing a trailer of campers at the hoedown

ca. 1971 Peter Burgdorff was one of the first barefooters at Camp

1974 Cabin 1 with counselor Brian O'Halleron, Jamie Bollinger, Kurt Reidel, Larry Wold, Rich Coomber, Scott MacDonald, Jim Risedorph, and counselor Rick Tozzie

1977 Chris and Lindsay Cole with son Jamie

THE SCHULZE & COLE YEARS (1976-80)

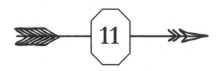

After John Bower, there were a series of Owatonna Directors, six over the next 14 years, from 1976 through 1989. The first was Bruce Schulze, who was Director for one season in 1976. He was a 1969 graduate of Springfield College and had a background working with Boy Scout camps and the YMCA. Before directing Owatonna, he directed an outdoor education program for public schools in Westfield, Massachusetts.[281] During Schulze's year in 1976, there was experimentation with dividing activity periods by ability level rather than by age divisions.[282] That year also marked the beginning of a golden era for the Golds team. After not winning Team Competition since their debut in 1968, the Golds earned four consecutive 1st-place finishes from 1976 to '79, which remains the longest streak in Camp history. The team captains during these years were Darren LePage, John Bullock, and two-time winner Jim Herberich, who would achieve impressive athletic accomplishments after his camp years.

Wells Sampson remembers Herberich, who was an older student in his hometown Sunday School in Winchester, Massachusetts.[283] At Camp, he made an impression on the younger Sampson, who took note of the long row of shoes lined up under Herberich's bunk: soccer cleats, tennis shoes, L.L.Bean boots, hiking boots, flip flops—one for every sport! If the shoes were any indication, Herberich was an all-round athlete. He had a long stride that made him uncatchable in games of Capture the Flag, and the Golds under his leadership seemed unbeatable. Herberich attended Phillips Andover Academy, and then went on to set track records in the 200 (20.78) and 400 (47.21) at Harvard University. In 1987, he began bobsledding competitively. Impressively, he made the U.S. Olympic team and competed in the 1988 Calgary, 1994 Lillehammer, and 1998 Nagano Olympic games, his best finish being 7th in the two-man event at Nagano.[284]

After Bruce Schulze, the next Director was Paul Christian "Chris" Cole for four seasons, from 1977 through '80. Cole was originally from Tulsa, Oklahoma. He was a Principia graduate, and he had been an instructor at Principia College in 1972 and '73. He then served three years in the U.S. Army as a Christian Science Chaplain from 1974 to '77, receiving survival training as a member of the Airborne Rangers, which is a rare qualification for a chaplain to achieve. He was fresh out of the Army when he became Director of Owatonna.[285]

Jamie Bollinger was a first-year counselor in 1977, and he remembers Cole sharing an Army story about calmly praying through a parachute jump that went wrong; the story left Bollinger feeling inspired to take on his new role as a counselor that summer.[286] Another sense of the tone Cole set is caught in a 1978 pre-camp letter that he sent to the staff with that year's metaphysical theme on "peaceful coexistence":

Christian Science gives us the most practical basis for being of one Mind, all in accord, ready to build together. It seems the biggest challenge is to love, understand, and even forgive those who are working closest to us. The success of our summer will be in proportion to our living of the great commandment Jesus taught us—the fulfillment of all law (Mark 12:28-31).[287]

During Cole's four years, enrollment remained high in the 90s, filling the 16 camper cabins. With the fashion of the 1970s in full swing, staff uniforms were updated with oversized but trendy (at the time) collars. New activities offered during this time included bicycling, as well as a more robust soccer program under the direction of "soccer director" Chic Johnson, who offered a two-week clinic at the end of camp.[288]

Johnson was also a C.I.T. counselor that summer, along with Jeff Robertson. During early mornings, it was common to see their C.I.T.s portaging canoes from the Boat Dock up to the flagpole and back down, as they trained for their Allagash River trip.[289] Other trips that summer included a Scouts' excursion to Mt. Chocorua, white-water canoeing down the Androscoggin, and a Boston trip that included stops at Mary Baker Eddy's historic house in Lynn, the Mother Church, and the Mary Beecher Longyear mansion in Chestnut Hill.[290]

Another highlight from Cole's first summer was the debut of a new Hydrodyne ski boat. This was in response to a survey from April 1977 that found that waterskiing was the most popular sport at Owatonna by a margin of 3 to 1; a call for a new boat and motor was put out and an effort made to "upgrade the waterskiing activity and make it one of unquestionable EXCELLENCE!!!"[291]

Jamie Bollinger remembers that his own father had supplied Camp with ski boats and water equipment up to that point, but it was John "Jack" Schlueter who procured the Hydrodyne.²⁹² It was Camp's first competition-level boat, and it would remain in operation until the early 1990s.²⁹³

Schlueter was a longtime counselor and Boat Master whose first year on staff was in 1966 and last was in 1983.²⁹⁴ "He imbibed Camp," is how Bollinger describes Schlueter, who he says could get the entire camp laughing with his renditions of the Maine comedy routine "Bert & I."²⁹⁵ In addition to getting the Hydrodyne, Schlueter is credited with introducing windsurfing as an activity. The Owatonna Yacht Club also thrived under Schlueter. The exclusive club was for Warriors and Chiefs who achieved a certain skill level in both sailing and canoeing. Once admitted, a card-carrying member could invite a Newfound girl to a private lobster bake. Scott Moeller went on his first ever date (at the tender age of 13) to the Yacht Club dinner.²⁹⁶ Jamie Bollinger strategically invited a girl who didn't like lobster, so that he could have two lobster dinners that night!²⁹⁷

It was also during Cole's first summer in 1977 that a local 4-mile road race was first run to both celebrate the Fourth of July holiday and benefit the Bridgton Public Library.²⁹⁸ Known as 4 on the Fourth, it was created by local residents Phoebe and Jerry Levine. Among the 28 runners in that first year was a group of counselors from Owatonna, including Larry Wold, Don Seymour, Jamie Bollinger, Rich Coomber, and Chic Johnson.²⁹⁹

Sometime in the early 1980s, all of Owatonna and Newfound began running the race, too. In 2003, the Camp Cup was established for runners representing the different local camps. The Cup is awarded to the camp with the best combined time of their top five campers. As of 2021, Owatonna has won the Camp Cup every year since its inception.³⁰⁰

1977 Stuart Jenkins, Don Seymour, Rich Coomber, and Chic Johnson at the first 4 on the Fourth Road Race

Cole's Assistant Director in 1979 was Peter Martin, who would eventually become Director himself a decade later. During this summer, Martin created a relay race called the Great Race, which came with its own tagline: "The Great Race is Truly Great!" It was an event he had first seen while working in 1977 at Camp Sunapee for Boys, a camp in New London, New Hampshire, run by Principia alumni Tony and Betty Shays.[301] His version at Owatonna pitted the four teams against each other, with every camper required to play a part in advancing their team.

The Great Race has evolved somewhat over the years. For example, during the 1980s, the "batons" were colored t-shirts that were worn and exchanged throughout the race.[302] Through the 1990s, the first event was always a 2-mile bike ride from Harrison to Owatonna, which changed in 2001 to a 1-mile run, and in 2002 to a 2-mile run from Harrison.³⁰³ Today, the race involves over 30 events, including bed-making, crab-walking, and s'more-roasting. One of the more notorious legs is when teams hand-paddle their canoe around Cherry Island—it is the great equalizer that has been known to send a 1st-place team into last place! The race culminates with a half-mile run up the Beach Trail and down the Truck Trail, after which all the teams celebrate together, a display that showcases Owatonna's strong sense of sportsmanship and brotherhood. And in a nod to Owatonna's regard for tradition, the race in recent years has been run by Program Director Duncan Wilder, who is the nephew of Peter Martin.

Cole's last season was 1980. He would go on to run his own education consulting company while also continuing to give Bible seminars.³⁰⁴ He was an adventurer at heart, a friend later recalled; tragically, Cole passed on in a motorcycle accident in 1999.³⁰⁵ A sense of his time at Owatonna is felt in a note he wrote to the campers at the end of his second season as Director:

> Thank you for your part in making 1978 a wonderful summer of camping on Long Lake. The council fires, trips, competition against other camps, and cabin nights are just a few of the memories we cherish. Owatonna challenges us. It shows us we can do a little better and a little more than we thought. Let us not forget the importance of our daily Bible lesson sermon in providing the basis for expressing this God given dominion and joy. Strive for excellence, be alert to the needs of others, and have a great year.³⁰⁶

1978 Hiking the Baldface Circle Trail

1978 Joint Newfound-Owatonna talent show

1984 Anita and Burt Cady, with children Allison and Chris

THE CADY YEARS
(1981-84)

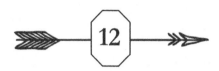

After Chris Cole, Burton "Burt" Cady became Director, filling the role for four years from 1981 to '84. Cady was a native of Massachusetts, and perhaps the first Director to have also been a camper. He'd been in the Senior division—and was a Blue—for two summers, back in 1960 and '61 during Phil Edwards's years. He thinks his mother may have sent him there as a way to cope with the loss of his father, who had passed away a couple years earlier. Later in 1968, Cady graduated from the University of Massachusetts, Amherst, then served two years as an officer in the U.S. Army. After a stint with the accounting firm Haskins & Sells, he became a middle school and high school math teacher in Walpole, Massachusetts, a career that lasted 38 years from 1972 to 2010.[307]

The tone Cady set for Camp is captured in a 1982 camp advertisement that promised to cultivate brotherhood, teamwork, and "spiritual muscle" through the application of Christian Science.[308] He brought his passion for education to his role as Director. Wells Sampson was a counselor at the time and remembers how Cady emphasized training, organization, and learning. Counselors were sent to pre-season clinics, activity areas all had curriculums, and campers could track their progress on well-maintained skill charts.[309] Jamie Bollinger was the Head Tripper in 1981, and he remembers Cady was a "good guy and a good Director. He was a math and numbers guy who also made sure nobody ever spent much! He did, however, approve the purchase of Camp's very first tents—two for Owatonna and two for Newfound."[310]

Cady made some changes to activities. For example, he relocated Owatonna's canoe program from operating out of the Boat Dock to the Newfound canoe beach—a change no doubt welcomed by the boys.[311] Although it had been offered previously, lacrosse was reinvigorated under Cady, who remembers specifically that one potential camper chose not to attend Camp because it lacked a lacrosse program. So, Cady started one up. Even more ambitious, he also added a computer programming elective one summer! "Not so sure how successful that one was," he reflected decades later.[312]

It was during these years that one of Owatonna's more well-known alumni was a camper. Zack Snyder was captain of the Reds in 1981 and '82. He would go on to become a Hollywood director, known for films such as *Dawn of the Dead* (2004), *300* (2006), and *Batman v Superman* (2016). While it is rumored that Snyder always finds a way to include the sound of a loon call in his films, it is confirmed that Snyder has a tattoo of the word *RED* on his forearm, a nod to his Owatonna team.

In 1983, Cady approved an unusual arrangement regarding Council Fire. Although the counselors that portray the various characters attempt to conceal their involvement, it's generally not too difficult for the campers to figure out who is who. But in 1983, only the most discerning campers could have figured out that Rich Coomber and Don MacKenzie were among them.

Neither were working at Camp that summer—they weren't even living in the same state! Coomber flew himself every weekend from Washington, D.C., to Portland, and MacKenzie drove up from Boston, picking Coomber up en route and making it to Camp in time for certain "unmentionable" Saturday night activities. "Counselors never admit to anything about Council Fire," said Rich Coomber, still maintaining the mystery 40 years later.[313]

Many campers today are familiar with the name Coomber Stadium, the soccer field behind the Warriors and Chiefs cabins. The field, of course, gets its name from Rich, who was a football placekicker at Williams College in Massachusetts. While working as a counselor in 1981, he began practicing his kicking in his spare time on the field. He explains:

> I built goal posts on the field with help from Erv Baker, who let me borrow some of his tools. I built these goal posts out of pipe—one was regular-sized and one was half sized. I'd be out there most days practicing, and kids and counselors would come and go shag balls for me, or they'd want to be my ball holder.[314]

When campers weren't available, Coomber used a one-of-a-kind camp-made football holder. It was engineered out of a turkey baster from the Owatonna kitchen, a coffee can, a Peak 1 stove case from the Trip Shack, and an upside-down scuba mask! Coomber kept up this routine for several summers, which first helped him make the All-New England 1st Team for Division III, and then led to chasing bigger dreams. When he returned to be a tripper in 1984, he left in the middle of the summer because he was signed as a placekicker for the Houston Oilers. He went to their training camp but was ultimately cut

1984 Coomber with his camp-made football holder

from the team. Fortunately, there was enough time to get back for the last weeks of Camp.

That was also Cady's last summer as Director. When he noticed that he was the last staff member to arrive during pre-season—because of his classes at Walpole High School—he realized the camp schedule and his teaching schedule were no longer in alignment.[315] He did return the next couple summers, though, to help out at Family Camp and promote enrollment for Owatonna.

THE CLARK, CRANDELL, & MARTIN YEARS (1985-89)

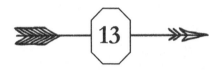

For the second half of the 1980s, Camp saw three different Directors assume the role. Bob Clark was in charge for a single summer in 1985. Like his predecessors, Clark was an educator who loved working with Christian Science youth. He worked at the Daycroft School throughout the 1980s, eventually becoming Headmaster there until it closed in 1991.[316] Later, he became Headmaster of Principia Upper School, before moving to Florida, where he became a Christian Science practitioner and served as the Christian Science Committee on Publication for the state.

During that 1985 summer, Rich Coomber was back working as a tripper, and he remembers taking a memorable trip out with the C.I.T.s to canoe the Allagash River and hike Mt. Katahdin. In those days, the trips program—or at least its equipment—was a bit less refined than what is offered today. Coomber says cotton was the clothing of choice and filtered water was not yet a thing. When it came to food, they often relied on Pop Tarts, and whoever was stuck lugging around the ginormous cans of beef stew had clearly drawn the short straw. Another memorable trip in 1985 was when Coomber helped arrange for a special visitor during one Braves trip to Mt. Chocorua. As the young campers were up on the mountain, a certain character in Native American attire emerged from the woods a few hundred yards below the summit, which surely gave the young boys something to talk about on the ride home or perhaps even a team-point winning nature report![317]

After Bob Clark, Gary Crandell took over from 1986 through '87. A self-described farm boy from Indiana, Crandell had graduated from Principia College in 1964 and then became a house pop as well as coach at Principia Upper School, where he stayed for most of his career.[318] Although never a camper, he came to Owatonna in 1968 to be Head Counselor, and then in 1969 to serve as John Bower's Assistant Director.

Dave Pelton was a counselor during Crandell's second year as Director. He remembers that summer there was a really unique joint Newfound-Owatonna sailing trip. Pelton, along with his cousin Greg Moore, Annie Thayer, and Wells Sampson—all experienced sailors—captained four boats out of Camden, Maine, and sailed for three days out on the ocean.[319]

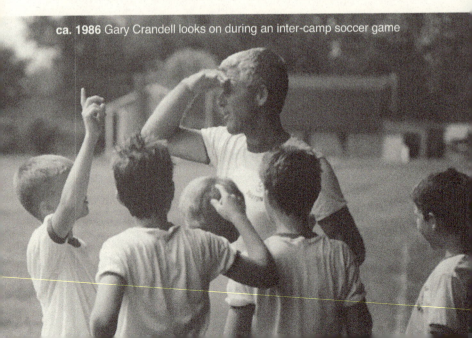

ca. 1986 Gary Crandell looks on during an inter-camp soccer game

Fourteen-year-old Brad Jealous also went on a memorable hiking trip up Mt. Brother in Baxter State Park at this time, which he detailed in a newsletter a decade later. There were four counselors on the trip, including Jamie Bollinger and Randy Green. During Green's time in the U.S. Air Force, he had come across the coordinates of a C-54 Skymaster (TWA Flight 277) that had crashed just southeast of Mt. Brother in 1944. Off into the woods they went to find the crash site, navigating by compass through dense brush. Jealous writes:

> Just about the time we were all ready to throw in the towel and head back to the campsite, we spotted some wreckage. We went on to find most of the airplane strewn in a line just below the peak of Fort Mountain. We came across the landing gear, old wooden propellers, and lots of aluminum fuselage. All of a sudden our outing had turned into a real adventure. The counselors literally had to pull us away from the site so that we had time to gain our bearings and retrace our steps back to the trail which would lead us to our campsite.[320]

Another unique tidbit from Crandell's second summer is that it is the only time the official all-camp photo was taken outside of Camp. Indeed, if you look through the Owatonna Lodge, the photo for 1987 shows about 50 campers and 20 staff dressed for the beach—Popham Beach. Visits to Popham were usually a highlight of the summer and were always an impressive demonstration of mass mobilization.[321]

Organizationally, two significant events occurred in the mid-1980s. The first was the merging together of Newfound and Owatonna into a single corporation with a shared Board of Trustees.[322] The second was the beginning of what would become a more drawn-out challenge, when in 1986 the Town of Harrison refactored land values, which created a sharp increase in shore-front property valuations.

In 1992, Newfound and Owatonna formally requested an abatement to reduce their owed property taxes, which turned into a question of constitutionality that played out in the courts over several years.[323] Initially, the trial judge ruled in Camp's favor, but then the Maine Supreme Judicial Court overruled in favor of the Town of Harrison. In 1994, the Board of Trustees, with much guidance from trustee member and attorney Lindsey Gorman, decided to appeal the case, going all the way up to the U.S. Supreme Court. The outcome was highly anticipated by many non-profit organizations across the country. In May 1997, by a vote of 5 to 4, the Supreme Court ruled in favor of Camp, which then received a tax refund and was exempted from all future property taxes. Camp continues to be grateful to be located in Harrison and makes an annual donation to the Town in that regard.[324]

Throughout all that, Camp continued to operate and expand as usual. During Crandell's years, a new ropes course was installed along the Boat Dock trail.[325] And sometime between 1986 and 1992, a street hockey court was laid next to the basketball court. This court did not yet have the tall side boards that stand today. Instead, there were shin-high wooden boards that kept the ball from rolling off the court but couldn't do anything to stop an airborne "wrister."[326]

After Gary Crandell wrapped up his time as Director, Peter Martin finished out the decade from 1988 to '89. Originally from Pennsylvania, Martin had grown up attending Camp, starting in 1965 and eventually captaining the Greens in 1970. He was on staff through the 1970s and '80s, including two years as Chris

1989 Marcia and Peter Martin

Cole's Assistant Director. His first year as Director was his 16th summer at Owatonna. Outside of Camp, he was an educator, spending time at the Daycroft School, Leelanau School, and eventually at Principia, where he was a dorm counselor, soccer coach, P.E. instructor, and biology teacher.[327]

At Camp and as a Director, Martin was known for his sense of adventure and fun. Wells Sampson was a counselor during the 1980s and described Martin as a "larger-than-life athlete and personality who was great fun to be around." Chic Johnson had known Martin since their earliest days as campers, and he worked as Martin's Head Counselor. "He loved to play," says Johnson, "and he was very engaged in Camp life. He didn't run Camp from a distance—he was right in the middle of everything!"[328]

And Camp seemed to be right in the middle of his life, too. When he and his wife Marcia got married in 1979, their first adventure as newlyweds was to come right up to Maine to work the summer. During the summer of 1980, Marcia was pregnant with their first child, and she and Peter had a good laugh at the idea of the baby arriving right in the middle of Council Fire—Peter was playing one of the characters that year, so there was a chance he could've shown up to the delivery room in costume! Fortunately, this did not happen, and when their daughter Lara was born, there was a touching Owatonna reception the next day. Marcia recalls:

> Peter wrapped up Lara in a little blanket and brought her up to the flagpole. The C.I.T.s had picked flowers and made one bouquet for me and one for Lara. Peter took her around the flagpole all wrapped up, and there wasn't a sound. I wasn't able to walk up there, but I was watching from HQ with tears running down my cheek. It was such a moment![329]

Marcia says that the little blanket had been knitted by Phoebe Ann (Connor) MacKenzie, who had done so much to help start Owatonna in the 1950s. It is believed that Marcia Martin was the first person to give birth while on the Owatonna staff.[330]

1985 Banquet centerpiece by the Greens team, captained by Selby Eddy
(Selby Eddy Collection)

1980s Sunday inspection with Peter Martin (Selby Eddy Collection)

1980s Frisbee at Popham Beach (Selby Eddy Collection)

1980s Running up to flagpole (Selby Eddy Collection)

1980s Hikers ready to go (Selby Eddy Collection)

1991 Seth Johnson and wife Libby Hoffman with son Caleb

The Johnson, Taylor, & Bollinger Years

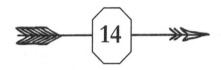

After two years as Assistant Director under Peter Martin, Seth "Chic" Johnson took on the Director role for the next four summers from 1990 through '93. Like Martin, Johnson also had grown up going to Owatonna, as his mother Connie Johnson was Newfound Director throughout the 1960s and '70s. Johnson's brothers Glenn, Clark, and later Todd were also campers; Glenn went on to become a counselor, C.I.T. counselor, and finally Head Counselor in 1971. Chic started as a Scout in Cabin 16 in the summer of 1964 and came back every year through 1970, finishing as a Chief. In those seven summers, he proved himself to be an exceptional athlete and received multiple feather awards.

He attended Williams College, where he captained both the soccer and hockey teams. Johnson eventually returned to Camp as a C.I.T. counselor in 1977, then worked as a team sports counselor in 1978 and '79. He returned again in 1988 and '89 as Peter Martin's Head Counselor before assuming the Director role. Professionally, Johnson was a soccer coach and athletics administrator. He worked at his alma mater Williams College, then was recruited by John Bower to coach at Principia College, where he spent 18 years from 1984 to 2002, eventually becoming Athletic Director.

As an athlete and coach, Johnson understood the educational value that comes through competition. In that regard, Camp had been an important developmental environment for him, because he remembers that they played a ton of inter-camp games when he was a camper. So when he became Director, he brought back this emphasis on competition and scheduled many matches against local camps like Wigwam, O-AT-KA, and Winona.[331]

Team Competition at Owatonna got a boost with the introduction of an intense new game called Flag Trip. The multi-day game of Capture the Flag is played in the woods and has become an annual fixture for specially selected Senior division campers. Matt Hoffman, who was Johnson's Head Counselor (and brother-in-law) in 1990 and '91, is credited with bringing the game over from Camp Leelanau.

Flag Trip was originally created by Leelanau trips counselors back in the 1950s.[332] They were looking for ways to make one of their trips to South Manitou Island more appealing to campers, and so they came up with their version of Capture the Flag. Campers would pack up canoes with supplies and paddle the eight miles out to the island. Each team operated out of the same well-established camping sites, where they lashed temporary structures out of wood and twine that were rated by judges; the ratings were factored in with the number of captured flags to determine the winner. In the 1980s, the trip moved from South Manitou to Al Hoffman's property, but today is played in various sites around Camp Leelanau.

At Owatonna, the game is played on Camp's woodland property on the other side of Route 35. Generally, the four teams are combined into two versus two. Flag Trip is considered by campers to be a significant factor in affecting the final point tallies of Team Competition.

During Johnson's four summers, a number of notable changes took place. New dark green uniforms were introduced, replacing the teal green shirts from Peter Martin's years. These dark greens have proven to be a long-term staple as they remain in use 30 years later. It was also during these years that two longtime fixtures said goodbye to Camp. One was the Hydrodyne boat that was retired in 1993 after 16 years of service—the boat had been acquired in 1977 and outlasted at least three outboard engines.[333] The other retirement was that of Head of Facilities Ervin Baker in 1990.

Baker had been with Owatonna for over three decades, longer than anyone else up to that point.[334] Generations of Owatonnans have fond memories of Erv and his wife, Pearl. Erv was especially known for his "Maine humor." Johnson remembers that when he was a young staff member in the 1970s, he was once helping Erv paint the Lighthouse bathroom, and

1988 Jamie Bollinger, Erv Baker, Rich Coomber

the bugs were really bad that morning. When he mentioned this to Erv, the old Mainer replied dryly that the bugs must have missed the "Bugs Keep Out" sign he had posted.[335] Jamie Bollinger says that he thought of Erv like a second father, and that Erv went out of his way to actually get to know campers. When asked about his memories of Pearl, who was Owatonna's beloved baker, Bollinger is instantly taken back to the inviting aroma wafting down from the kitchen. "Oh my gosh, those cinnamon buns! You'd wake up smelling those things!"[336]

Another change was the replacement of 13 of the 16 camper cabins with nine new ones. This decision was a bit controversial. One concern was about the size of the cabins: the old cabins were smaller and thought to foster a closer group dynamic with fewer campers and a single counselor; the new cabins were larger, allowing for more boys and two counselors per group. A separate concern was about how to preserve the history of the old cabins, which were covered on the inside with names graffitied by generations of campers. Jamie Bollinger remembers successfully advocating for at least leaving the original Scouts cabins untouched. He also personally cut out many of the handwritten names from the old cabins, which were then able to be used as fundraising gifts, many of them now hanging on the walls of the new cabins. After the new Braves cabins were built, it was acknowledged that they were in fact a bit large, and so the dimensions for the subsequent Warriors and Chiefs cabins were downsized.[337]

Regardless of the changes made under Seth Johnson, in most ways Camp remained much the same. As always, Christian Science remained at the heart of the mission. An April 1990 "identity statement" listed at the top of eight bullets that Camp was "where Christian Science is lived and loved" and "where a healing atmosphere is provided recognizing no lack or limitation."³³⁸

Chic Johnson wrapped up his time as Director in 1994 when he was named Athletic Director at Principia College. He continued at Principia for another eight years before moving to Maine in 2003, where he coached at Bates College, in club soccer, and as an Olympic Development coach. From 2006 to 2011, he served as the Christian Science Committee on Publication for the state. Johnson would eventually become the Executive Director of both camps in April 2015, a role that he continues to serve in as of 2021.³³⁹

Succeeding Johnson as Director in 1994 was David Taylor, who ran Camp for the next three summers through 1996. Born in England but raised in Boston, Taylor had been a camper in the 1960s and a counselor in the '70s. He'd spent time working

1975 Dave Taylor as a counselor

as a resident counselor at Principia College, then later became a high school history teacher in Southern California. Taylor had a jovial spirit, and wherever he went, hilarious stories seemed to follow.

One challenge as Director that Taylor remembers—with more amusement now than at the time—was in finding and retaining a reliable Head Cook. During his first summer, his cook quit after two weeks, forcing Dave to scramble for a replacement. He and his wife Janet, a new mother at the time, ended up working the grill themselves. At one point, Taylor resorted to hiring a colorful Spaniard named Gabriel. One morning a few minutes before breakfast, Taylor panicked when he realized there were no lights on in the kitchen, the kitchen boys were still sleeping, and Gabriel was nowhere to be found—he'd gone AWOL and wasn't heard from for several days! These lessons from the kitchen served Taylor well when he would return to Camp to be Head Cook himself in the early 2000s.[340]

In Taylor's first year, the Scouts cabins were rearranged into a cluster and united by a shared deck, known as the Scouts Porch.[341] By Taylor's last year, the Board of Trustees began envisioning a series of more substantial renovations to Camp, as many of the structures had grown old. In May 1996, it was announced that Peter Whitchurch, a Christian Scientist from Florida, would become a year-round Head of Facilities to oversee 60 buildings, 10 vehicles, and 160 acres of grounds.[342] Whitchurch's background is captured in a 2014 *Call of the Loon* article written by his daughter Jill:

> My dad's eclectic resume was perfect for this position. His education was in forestry and wildlife management. He owned and managed car washes for 14 years, which provided him with an understanding of machinery and

water systems. While working for Florida's Department of Natural Resources as a biologist, he designed and built a fish tagging contraption. And one of Dad's hobbies was woodworking, so he had skills in carpentry and building.[343]

Whitchurch would spend the next 19 years working for both Newfound and Owatonna, and in that time he and his team completed countless projects and improvements. When he started in 1996, he immediately began a series of projects that would take a few years to finish; some of these included replacing building foundations, replacing the docks and swim floats, and upgrading water, plumbing, and electrical systems.[344]

Forrest Bless and Reid Charlston, both future Owatonna Directors, were campers during the 1990s. Highlights for them include some epic camping trips. Bless remembers a biking trip through scenic Acadia National Park, and a sailing trip on an America's Cup boat with counselor Bart Spaulding. One summer, there was even enough snow on top of Mt. Jefferson in the Presidential Range to have a snowball fight, which was also the first time camper Mark Clark had ever seen snow! Charlston remembers a trip with counselor Kevin "Cuz" Kozin to Ram Island, off the coast of Portland. They camped out there in the fog and to pass the time, Cuz taught the boys how to swing dance, promising them it would be a hit with their Newfound co-eds![345]

As a counselor later in the 2000s, Charlston developed a signature look for his long orange dreadlocks and his collection of frisbees. The origin of the dreads is a mystery, but his love of frisbee came from his three summers as a camper in the mid-1990s. One of these summers was particularly rainy, and Ultimate Frisbee became his favorite rainy-day activity. He also remembers witnessing an incredible athletic feat involving counselor Josh Burek chasing down a frisbee. Burek, who was an All-American decathlete at Principia College in 1999, stood a few yards behind Dave Steckler on one end of Coomber Stadium; with a running start, Burek passed Steckler just as Steckler launched a frisbee across the field; Burek then chased down that frisbee, running what seemed to Charlston to be the entire length of the field and diving off the back to make the catch![346]

Forrest Bless remembers his own moment of athletic glory during a nail-biting Team Day in 1998 when he was a Chief. It was the Golds versus the Reds in the lacrosse final, and Bless was put in as the Golds' goalie, a position and a sport he had never played before. The Reds were stacked that year with five C.I.T.s, but Bless turned out to be a natural goaltender, shutting down his opponents' attempts to score. It was an epic match that went into double overtime and eventually saw the Golds take the victory with a final goal from captain Charlie Ronemus. Bless remembers going home to Vermont after that summer with a newfound conviction to start a lacrosse team with his friends.[347]

After David Taylor, Jamie Bollinger became Director in 1997 and held the position through 1999. Bollinger, a Florida native, spent seven years as a camper, starting as a Scout in 1967 and ending as a C.I.T. in 1975. Camp has always been his "home away from home," he says, but it was almost his permanent home, according to a humorous family anecdote. His parents brought him along for a visit to Camp when he was still a baby. As they got caught up in conversations with friends walking down to the Beach, they accidentally left Bollinger in his bassinet up on the Owatonna rock! Thankfully, Phil Edwards noticed and carried him down to be reunited with his parents.[348]

Bollinger was a waterski counselor in 1977 and '78, then returned in 1981 as Head Tripper. In 1983, after longtime counselor Jack Schlueter hung up his skis, Bollinger became Boat Master, a position he held through 1987. Countless Owatonna alumni credit Bolo with getting them up on skis, but interestingly when he was a boy, he didn't want anything to do with skiing! It took a patient and creative counselor named Andy Rodgers to help Bollinger learn to ski, by pulling him back and forth without a boat along the Owatonna Beach. That was the start of Bollinger's lifelong love of waterskiing, a passion that he has passed onto many Owatonna campers since.[349]

In the early 1990s, Bollinger came back to Camp as the Director of Enrollment, a new position that focused exclusively on recruiting more campers. Despite his efforts flying around the country talking up a summer on Long Lake, petering numbers continued to be a challenge for several years. He got the chance to really tackle the problem when he became Owatonna's first year-round Director in 1997, meaning he could spend the offseason recruiting campers and staff for the next season. It paid off, and by his second summer, he remembers they enrolled over 100 boys, which he thinks hadn't been done since perhaps John Bower's era nearly 30 years earlier.

Bollinger's Senior Staff included his longtime friend Chris "Skip" Schneider. Together, they brought back a number of activities that had once been Owatonna staples. The Track Meet, for example, had for many years been run around a track that was once located where Coomber Stadium is today. That track had been removed by this time, so Bollinger and Schneider made arrangements to hold the event at nearby Fryeburg Academy, where it continues to be held today. They brought the Hill Run back, too, as well as evening activities like Gitchi-Gumi. With the Water Carnival, it was decided to change the competition away from Owatonna versus Newfound and instead divide both camps into their respective four teams.

Bollinger summarized their approach to all these activities in an August 1999 newsletter: "Extra emphasis was put on experiencing true competition, which we defined as giving of yourself while striving for your best effort, so that your opponent can perform his/her best."[350] Other reports paint a picture of the bountiful good from that summer, too. A visually-impaired camper appreciated the supportive atmosphere that helped him climb to the top of the rock wall and waterski off the boom half way across Long Lake. Three Scouts completed the Atomic Cherry Swim, which is a swim *around* Cherry Island. Two Chiefs pushed each other on the Hill Run and ended up both recording a time of 1:39, beating the old record by 12 seconds.[351]

Several building projects also took place at this time. They may have been possible largely due to some good news that came just before the start of Bollinger's first summer: the United States Supreme Court ruled in favor of Newfound and Owatonna's tax lawsuit.[352] Later that same year, Owatonna announced a 10-year capital campaign, in which it sought to raise funds and restore many of its old buildings, as well as build new ones. A 40-foot-tall climbing wall located next to the archery range was constructed, and a 65-foot-long zipline was built, running from a tree by the climbing wall and across the hill towards HQ.[353]

Several old buildings were replaced and then repurposed. A much-needed New Lighthouse bathroom was built at the bottom of the grove in 1998; the Old Lighthouse was then moved behind the Lodge and cut into two staff cabins.[354] Where the Old Lighthouse had been, a new woodshop was built in 1999 (which today is now the Pavilion). Just beyond the New Lighthouse, a new C.I.T. cabin was built.[355] Another repurposed building was the old Scouts bathroom, Dreamland. Bollinger recalls:

> I figured the building couldn't be that heavy, so we lined up the entire staff and carried it to its new location as a "trunk" room for Cabin 0. The staff continued to remind me throughout that summer that it was much heavier than "I" thought it would be.[356]

After the 1999 season, Bollinger stepped down from being Director and joined the Owatonna Board of Trustees for several years. He's returned since then to teach ski clinics and lead the trips program. In 2011, Bonnie Bower stepped down as Executive Director and Bollinger assumed the position, which he held until 2015. Bollinger has been a presence and a helping hand at Camp for decades, and he has watched as his own three boys grew up there. With a nearby house on Long Lake, he remains just a short boat ride away from his home away from home.

2009 Alumni Field, also known as Coomber Stadium

2003 Travis and Hannah Brantingham

The Martin, Brantingham, & Frank Years

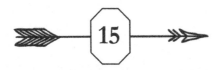

Peter Martin returned to be Director in 2000 and '01. He'd been Head Tripper under Jamie Bollinger in the 1990s, but he had also been Director previously in the 1980s. This second stint makes him the only person so far to have held the position at two separate times.

In that first summer, Martin and counselor Dave Steckler created the Arrowhead award.[357] Martin explained in a note to parents: "This special honor recognizes a camper's overall contribution to Camp through his consistent expression of the qualities of the Christ in his daily actions."[358] He included examples of several recent citations: "For expressing consistent joy and love toward each of his cabin-mates"; "For his relentless unselfishness, constant enthusiasm, and ever willingness to listen and cooperate while on the Magalloway River canoeing trip"; "For great progress in the past week—he has persevered and overcome past challenges to let his true self shine through." Arrowheads are awarded once a week before Saturday dinner. Repeat recipients add beads painted in team colors to their necklace, and every five beads is replaced with a "bear claw."

Enrollment continued to be high at this time, with the 2000 season numbering 112 campers, requiring the Trips program to send out a record-breaking 15 excursions during Second Session.[359] Perhaps it was these higher numbers that led Dave Steckler to redesign the program for the next summer in 2001.[360] In the early Owatonna years, trips went out every other Monday; eventually, they went out "shotgun-style" with all the campers away at the same time, once per session. Steckler's new system sent trips out by age division, ensuring that Camp was never completely empty and facilitating a smoother planning process.[361] Trip highlights from the summer of 2000 included: a 135-mile bike ride from the Quebec border in Beecher Falls, Vermont, back to Owatonna; a photography trip to Acadia National Park; and a climbing trip to Rumney, New Hampshire, very close to where Mary Baker Eddy lived in the 1860s.[362]

Building projects, funded by the capital campaign that began in 1997, continued under Martin's tenure. In 2000, the climbing wall was renovated to now include a more challenging reverse (chimney) incline section. The Owatonna kitchen and the arts and crafts building were also expanded around this time.[363] Out on the water, a new Malibu ski boat, rigged with a Wedge and Skylon, allowed for the addition of wakeboarding to the Boat Dock offerings.[364] The street hockey court was upgraded in 2000, too, with new boards to line the sides of the court.[365] Future Owatonna Director Travis Brantingham remembers the project was a memorable demonstration of Christian Science prayer.

The boards were generously donated and manufactured by brothers Peter and Tracy Switzer, but they needed to be hauled from St. Louis to Maine. Peter Switzer, Jamie Bollinger, and camp parent Jim Stock volunteered to make the drive. They loaded up a rickety old trailer with the boards, but they also piled on donated stacks of Christian Science periodicals and sets of Olympic weights. Bollinger remembers they blew out all four of the trailer's tires during the road trip. They were also pulled over in Ohio, although they were let off after the policeman spoke to Pete Whitchurch by phone. They assembled the new boards in a weekend and then made the drive back to St. Louis.[366]

At the behest of former Owatonna Director and now Principia Headmaster Bob Clark, Peter Martin decided to return to the school after the 2001 season. There, he was a beloved P.E. instructor at the Lower School. He often drew from his Camp experiences by implementing innovative programs that blended fun and character education, such as one called Project Adventure. He explained in a 2009 school publication: "Adventure refers to the way things are done—it means we include an element of something new or surprising in an activity so that there's opportunity for self-discovery."[367] Martin's philosophy certainly continues to live on at both Principia and Owatonna.

In 2002, Travis Brantingham became Director, a role he held for the next five years through 2006. Brantingham had been a camper for one summer in 1990. His mom had signed him up without asking him, but he ended up having a blast—one highlight being an epic biking trip through the White Mountains. He returned to Owatonna in the late 1990s as the Waterfront Director and then as Head Counselor under Jamie Bollinger. Although just 22-years old, Brantingham was first offered the position of Director in 2000, but then it was discovered that he was not yet old enough according to ACA regulations. So, he spent two influential summers at Camp Leelanau as Assistant

Director for Clark Shutt, a highly respected educator and longtime Leelanau Director.[368]

Once old enough at age 25, Brantingham returned to Owatonna as Director. His vision for Camp was defined by three mottos that he adapted from his time at Leelanau: *Be the Best*, *Love One Another*, and *Have Fun*. He had these mottos carved into plaques and hung up prominently in the Lodge. A fourth motto, *Give Gratitude*, was added later, its plaque hung intentionally over the door to the kitchen. Together, these have become known as Owatonna's Four Pillars, ideals for every camper and counselor to live by each summer.

Brantingham wanted Owatonna, its staff, and its campers to be the best that they could be, which, by doing so, would get at its mission to serve the Cause of Christian Science. This translated into an expectation of high standards in all of Camp's activities, and it followed that an elevated sense of competition permeated the programming. For example, Brantingham recalls that his Senior Staff figured out how many days were in a single summer, and then they scheduled "some ridiculous number" of inter-camp sports matches, so that there were sometimes two or three matches a day each week![369]

Evan MacDonald was the Program Director in 2004, which was a particularly high year for enrollment with approximately 120 campers. He remembers how busy it was because he personally drove the campers to nearly every away game. His handwritten schedule for First Session records 19 games over two weeks, with matches against Wigwam, O-AT-KA, and Winona in kickball, hockey, soccer, lacrosse, basketball, and Ultimate Frisbee. The increased competition was partly meant to appeal to athletic campers who might otherwise skip Owatonna for sports camps elsewhere. The main purpose, though, was to encourage all campers to break through their limitations, both human and spiritual.[370]

Brantingham resurrected and revitalized old activities, like Battleship and Gitchi-Gumi. While the Flag Trip had never gone away, Brantingham brought in two veteran players from Camp Leelanau—Bill Warrick and Charley Martin—to help organize and intensify the Owatonna game. He made the Track Meet an annual event again. Naturally, a plaque for track and field records was hung up in the Lodge, and the oldest record still on them was set in 2005. The Reds' Junior division 4x100 relay team, consisting of Ken Manning, Nate Waters, Timmy Bollinger, and Will Fetter, ran a time of 1:06.88, a record unbroken 16 years later.[371] In fact, the Reds were strong that summer, culminating in taking 2nd place, which set another record of sorts—it ended the longest "place drought" in Camp's history as the Reds had not finished in 2nd place since 1982.[372]

Another new-old program was Woodsman. Known as campcraft in earlier years, it was given new life when Brantingham made it a goal to bring it back in 2004. He asked counselors Mike Vernon and Aaron Morris to get the program off the ground, and a designated area was built for it out in the woods behind the baseball diamond.[373] The Woodsman Award was established, given to campers who completed the curriculum, sometimes over the course of multiple summers. It required the successful completion of a 24-hour solo in the woods, and it culminated in the camper planning and leading an actual camping trip. The first camper to get his name on the Woodsman plaque was Jeremy Robertson in 2004.

A new signature event created in these years was the Mountain Man Challenge. Brantingham remembers the exact moment the idea came to be:

Mike Vernon and I were standing on the Lodge porch and talking about the Tour de France. We were bantering about how cool the race was and how cool it would be to do something like that at Camp. We wanted to buy bikes for the campers, but there wasn't any money to do that. So, we thought, we can make 'em run![374]

The challenge that was created was a series of three races: the first, a short run up Hawk Mountain; a second slightly longer run up Mt. Pleasant; and, for those who qualify, a 9-mile run up and down Mt. Washington. The best overall time receives the Mountain Man Award, which has generally been a one-of-a-kind Owatonna athletic shirt. The top times are recorded on a plaque in the Lodge, the current record belonging to Silas Eastman with a time of 2:37:38 in 2010.

Some significant upgrades occurred during Brantingham's time. He says that in his first two years, they worked to replace most of Owatonna's sporting equipment. This was made possible with generous support from the beloved Boston sporting goods store City Sports, which happened to have two Owatonna connections: Co-founder Eric Martin was the parent of a camper, and Senior Buyer Erik Metzdorf was a former Reds team captain and counselor from the 1980s. Team Sports counselor Evan MacDonald remembers showing up to the City Sports warehouse and loading the camp van up with cases and cases of equipment—basketballs, volleyballs, hockey gear—it was an unforgettable shopping spree![375]

The biggest project that took place under Brantingham and was overseen by Pete Whitchurch was the re-grading of Coomber Stadium in 2004.[376] Brantingham remembers his pitch to the Board of Trustees was that Newfound's property is special because of its incredible waterfront; Owatonna's specialty is sports, and so it should have an incredible field. The new field was completed in the Fall of 2002.[377] As it had been made possible by the generous donations from many alumni, the field was renamed Alumni Field in their honor.

A number of service projects took place during these years, especially for the C.I.T. program. C.I.T.s from 2003 will fondly remember carrying lumber down the Beach Trail to construct a lean-to. A new and larger beach shack was constructed. The C.I.T.s in 2005 spent many early mornings building a new Junior Counselor cabin (later repurposed as HQ II) located behind the Scouts porch.

In 2006 Brantingham experimented with a revitalized Junior Counselor program. He again asked seasoned Leelanau counselors Bill Warrick and Charley Martin to lead the program, and six J.C.s were selected to participate. During First Session, the group developed leadership skills by completing a two-week canoeing trip 380 miles away in Canada's Algonquin State Park, perhaps the furthest away and longest wilderness trip taken out in Camp's history. It was an unforgettable experience but repeating it every summer proved unsustainable.

The 2006 J.C. program did leave a legacy in another way, as it led to the creation of the novel camp game Ultimate RPS. Warrick and Martin were experienced Rock-Paper-Scissors players who adhered to the International Rules version of the sport. Junior Counselors Spencer Holland and James Suber became avid students and eventually innovators, developing Ultimate RPS by incorporating traditional dueling conventions, notably a 5 or 10-step walk-off.

On a more impressive athletic note, 2006 saw C.I.T. Colin Anderson win the Triple Crown for captaining the Greens to 1st place and receiving both the White and Black Feathers. The longtime camper from Dallas, Texas, also happens to be the grandson of Owatonna's second Director, Ty Anderson. Colin was just the 6th camper to win the Triple Crown, the last being fellow Green Kenny Gray back in 1975. After Colin ended the 30-year drought, he would be followed by the Greens' Tony Bumatay in 2011, the Golds' Henry Howell in 2016, and the Greens' Wells Faulstich in 2019.[378]

When Brantingham was named Assistant Dean of Students at the Principia School in 2006, he stepped down from his role as Director of Owatonna. He continued his career in education at Principia, working as the Athletic Director, Principal, and finally as Head of School. Additionally, he served on Camp's Board of Trustees for two years. He recently transitioned into the private sector.

The next Director was Brandon Frank, who served in the position for four years from 2007 to 2010. Frank had worked on Brantingham's staff from 2002 to '05, which included time on Senior Staff and as a tripper. He first came to Owatonna because of Chic Johnson, who was Frank's soccer coach at Principia College. As a staff member, Frank recruited his entire family to come to Camp with him, including his younger brothers, sister, and even his mom, who worked as Camp Mom.[379]

During Frank's first year as Director, Owatonna made local headlines when counselor Erik Stanley won the 4 on the Fourth road race with a time of 19:57. Stanley had just wrapped up his junior year running at the University of Texas, where he had finished 10th at the NCAA championships.[380] In high school, Stanley had been ranked #1 in the nation for the mile with a time of 4:04.[381] This was his first year at Owatonna, and he maintained an impressive running routine despite the long days. When most counselors were just waking up, Stanley often was

2009 Brandon Frank (center) with his Senior Staff, Head Counselor Tyler Maltbie and Program Director Forrest Bless

just returning from a long-distance run. His win on July 4 was the first time an Owatonnan or Newfounder had won the race.[382] A few years later in 2012, Owatonna alum Silas Eastman—and still the record-holder for the Mountain Man Challenge—would win the race, too.

Facilities enhancements continued during these years as several buildings shifted around. In 2008, the Counselor Cabin that was located on the Newfound hill was renovated and winterized; it became Loon Lodge, a year-round office and home for the Executive Director. The Owatonna Director's cottage, located next to the laundry room, was repurposed to be the new Counselor Cabin. Finally, the Owatonna HQ building was renovated and expanded to house the Director and his family.[383] C.I.T. projects from these years added several more contributions, including a new Reading Room behind the Scouts Porch, a renovated Rec Hall with an added deck, a rebuilt archery shed, and even a garden up by the Newfound soccer field.

There was some creative experimentation with programming during Frank's tenure. "There will be more creativity and opportunity for individual choice," Frank wrote in a Spring 2008 issue of the *Call of the Loon*. "Campers can look forward to having special day trips, club afternoons, new evening activities, early morning ski time, and custom block periods for those campers striving to increase their ability in their favorite activity."[384]

Frank's last summer was in 2010. He now lives in Los Angeles with his wife and three children and is the President of Pacific Packaging Components, Inc.

2009 Flagpole on a Sunday

2009 Coming together to shout a "Fadada" team cheer

2008 Hitting bullseyes at the archery range

2009 Lined up by teams on Team Day

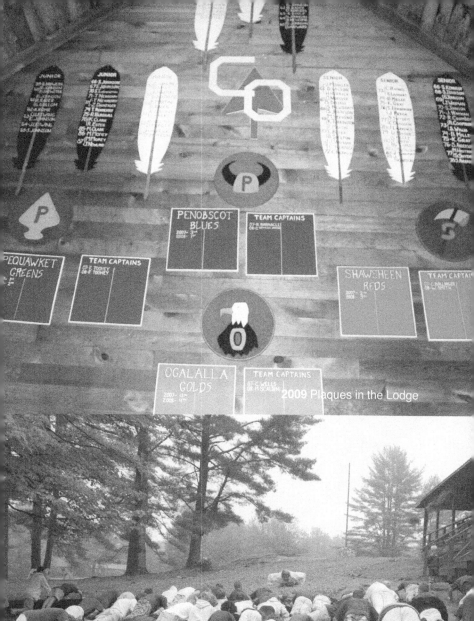

2009 Plaques in the Lodge

2008 The Counselor of the Day (C.O.D.) leads morning "callies"

2016 Aerial of the Owatonna grounds

2012 Johanna and Forrest Bless

THE BLESS, PELTON, & CHARLSTON YEARS

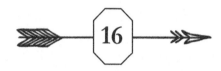

Forrest Bless became Director in 2011 and held the position for two years. Bless was a longtime Owatonnan with 16 summers under his belt by the time he became Director. His family was first introduced to Camp through his uncle Bill Shattuck, who had been sponsored to attend in the 1970s by the Director at the time, John Bower. Raised in Bristol, Vermont, Bless's first year was in 1993 as a nine-year-old, and he continued through his C.I.T. year in 2000. Travis Brantingham then recruited him to return as a counselor and tennis instructor in 2002. Eventually, Bless ran the rocks and ropes program before becoming a tripper, a Program Director, and the Assistant Director for two summers under Brandon Frank. Outside of Camp, Bless had graduated from Principia College in 2007, then worked a couple seasons at the Leelanau Outdoor Center and later at a sporting goods company.[385]

Inspired by his background teaching rocks and ropes, an area of focus for Bless as Director was to add more opportunities for campers to work on team building and the overcoming of personal fears. He had started some of this work when he was on Brandon Frank's Senior Staff by enhancing the offerings at the low ropes course. He continued this vision as Director and was able to expand the elements offered at the high ropes course in 2011.[386]

Another focus for Bless was providing experiences for campers and counselors to grow spiritually. He remembers that it had been at Camp where he first prayed for someone other than himself, which was a foundational moment for him. Additionally, when he was in college, he conducted an interesting independent research project that asked the question: What does it mean to serve the Cause of Christian Science? He interviewed individuals and dove into literature on the subject. Among his findings were that successful practitioners of the faith needed to be purpose-driven individuals, effective healers, and dedicated Church members. Camp, he believed, was an excellent environment—especially for counselors—to develop the very competencies needed to unselfishly serve the Cause, and so these were recurring themes he touched on as Director.[387]

One project undertaken by Head of Facilities Pete Whitchurch at this time was to address the slowly eroding Owatonna Beach. It had become a growing problem over the years, as runoff from the Beach Trail had begun to carve a sizeable canal into the downward sloping beach. As part of the solution, Whitchurch built a sand volleyball court behind the tree line above the beach.

In Team Competition, 2011 was another memorable year for the Greens as captain Tony Bumatay earned the Triple Crown, just five years after previous captain Colin Anderson had. Oddly, after this victory, the Greens would finish the next three summers in 2nd, 3rd, and 4th—the only time a team has regressed in that sequential order.[388] There was excellence on display in inter-camp competition, too. Evan MacDonald says Owatonna's victory over Wigwam in a 2012 street hockey game was one of the most incredible comebacks he's ever watched.[389] There had been some miscommunication that led Owatonna to bring U11 campers to play against Wigwam's older U13 team. Down 4 goals with minutes to go, Owatonna went on a scoring rampage, ultimately winning the game and leaving the older Wigwam boys stunned.

Forrest Bless wrapped up his time as Director after the 2012 season. He went on to be a marketing manager at The Christian Science Publishing Society in Boston, Massachusetts, for several years. Eventually, he returned to JumpSport, a family-owned sporting goods company in Northern California, and currently is its President.

In 2013, Dave Pelton became Director. Pelton had been a camper for six years in the 1970s and '80s. He spent one summer as a kitchen boy, was a windsurfing counselor in 1987 and '88, and was a C.I.T. counselor in '89. As a Principia College student, Pelton had been a successful decathlete, and after graduating, he continued to compete into the mid-1990s. Professionally, he had been working in the energy industry but was looking for a career change when the Director position opened up, and so he returned to Owatonna.[390]

Pelton is, of course, well known for being the songwriter of the beloved camp song, "My Owatonna Home Away From Home," which he wrote in 1997. Jamie Bollinger was the Director at the time, and Pelton was working as a songwriter and music producer in Nashville, Tennessee. When Bollinger realized that many of his staff were unfamiliar with singing old camp songs, he asked Pelton to visit during pre-camp training to teach them. Bollinger says:

> I remember Dave telling the staff about how "manly" it was to sing. He got their attention by telling them about when he was qualifying for Olympic Trials in the Decathlon—and bench pressing some insane amount, like 350 lbs. I could see all the guys sitting up in their chairs all of the sudden and REALLY excited to learn![391]

In preparation for the visit, Pelton wrote two new songs that he wanted to teach the counselors. He explains:

> When I was a C.I.T., there was a song that my counselor co-wrote along with some Scouts counselors, called "Here at Owatonna, Life is Really Out of Sight." It was a call-response song, and it was catchy. I thought that I should write an updated version of that song, so I wrote this really catchy, up-tempo song. Then I put that song aside, and a couple hours later, this other song popped into my head; it was a little slower, a little more melodic, a little more folky. Everything that I loved about Camp and that I remembered about Camp just came out.[392]

At the pre-camp session, Pelton taught both of his new songs, but it was the slower, folky song—"My Owatonna Home Away From Home"—that really stuck with the staff, and it has been sung every summer since!

Additionally, at the request of the Executive Director at the time, Amy Sparkman, Pelton produced a music album of camp songs. Recording these tunes ensured that they could not be forgotten by future generations. Camp alumni with professional music careers, such as Bill Burden, Lisa Redfern, and Mindy

2013 Dave Pelton leading songs at the final banquet

Jostyn, joined Pelton on some of the tracks. For the rendition of "Charlie on the M.T.A.," Pelton had former Directors Peter Martin and Jamie Bollinger sing along with him, and he called the track the "Director's Cut." Little did he know in 1997 that he himself would become Director later in 2013.[393]

A highlight of the 2013 summer was the construction of an outdoor amphitheater, located in the firebreak down below Coomber Stadium. It began as a Newfound C.I.T. project but naturally blossomed into a joint Newfound-Owatonna effort that included both C.I.T. groups, Junior and Senior division campers, and even the four teams.[394] The project had a profound impact on some campers. One parent was so touched by what it had meant to her son that she handed a check to Executive Director Jamie Bollinger at the end of the summer; the check happened to cover almost the exact amount of the cost of the materials for the project.[395]

Another project during Pelton's time was the building of a new Swim Shed down at the Owatonna Beach. With the wood from the old shed, they built a giant bonfire at the beach. The fire was so large and hot, Pelton remembers, that some frisbees that were thrown around the blaze partially melted in mid-flight![396]

These were some of the final projects completed by longtime Head of Facilities Pete Whitchurch. He retired after the 2014 season, having served Camp for 19 productive years. His daughter Jill wrote about Pete's career in an article for the *Call of the Loon*:

> When asked how long he has been at Camp, Dad says, "Long enough to wear out three trucks and two John Deere mowers." Highlights for Dad include cooking lobster and corn, driving the hay wagon at the socials, and teaching camp Sunday School. But his favorite thing was working with the C.I.T.s on their projects, especially the Newfound C.I.T.s, since this was the first opportunity many Newfounders had to use wood-working tools.... What stands out to me most is how his job required consistent patience, understanding, and humor, while he juggled working with folks from town, contractors, the camp staff and Board, campers, and the physical demands of a large property. My dad rose to the challenge with intelligence and grace.[397]

A year after Whitchurch's retirement, Pelton also stepped down from his role as Director in order to begin a career in real estate development. Camp is still his home away from home, as he splits his time between Nashville and Maine and has three kids who have been to Camp and Family Camp.[398]

2014 Pete Whitchurch on his trusty tractor

Reid Charlston became the next Director in 2016, a position he still holds six years later, the longest tenure since John Bower in the 1970s. When Charlston's mom, Shari, became a Christian Science nurse at Camp in 1995, the family tagged along. Charlston spent three summers as a camper, and then he came back as a counselor from 2002 to '09, often teaching kayaking and leading trips. He attended Principia all the way through, and after graduating in 2004, he worked as an athletic director and P.E. teacher at the Fox River Country Day School, a school in Chicago founded on Christian Science principles, before working several years as a resident counselor and in administration at Principia College.[399]

2009 Reid Charlston as a tripper

Explaining his path to becoming Owatonna Director, he says, "That was God." Without planning it, all his professional experiences up to that point prepared him for the role: he'd spent time in early education, time with college students, and time in administration. "I'd always been about working with young people and serving the Christian Science movement, and being Director was the coolest way to do that!"[400]

The biggest building project during Charlston's time was the Lodge renovation that was completed in 2017 between his first and second year. This included a remodel of the kitchen and rebuilding of the bathroom known as "Four on the Floor." A smaller project constructed later was "Tin City," an addition of four outdoor shower stalls to the back of the Lighthouse bathroom.

In 2020, for the first time in Owatonna's history, there was no summer season, due to the global COVID-19 pandemic. "It was really challenging to make that decision," said Charlston, "but in retrospect, we think it was the right decision."[401] The pandemic, of course, is still ongoing over a year later in 2021, and it has affected nearly every part of the globe in some way, especially with its restrictions on gathering and traveling.

Like Owatonna, many camps across the United States did not run programs in 2020. Charlston and Newfound Director Mary Rankin thought creatively about how to stay engaged with their campers and counselors. They recorded and sent personalized videos to every registered camper to say hello and tell them how much they were missed that summer. For the duration of Camp's usual seven-week session, Charlston and Rankin led weekly online morning meetings, which were well attended and allowed the entire Camp family to stay connected and uplifted during a difficult time.

After a year hiatus, Owatonna and Newfound did welcome campers back for a successful summer in 2021. As it has for 100 years, our home away from home was once again buzzing with activity. Boys were sprinting up to the flagpole, diving into Long Lake, and gathering around the campfire. They were learning to be their best, to love one another, to have a lot of fun, and to give gratitude for their many daily blessings. And they did it all with God above them and their brothers beside them.

Until we meet again…

2012 Joint Newfound-Owatonna concert in the Lodge

2011 The Green team's base in Flag Trip

2016 High ropes course

2016 Joint Sunday School at Newfound

2016 Lowering the flag at the end of a full day

Appendix

Directors

Camp Ropioa
1922-1934	George A. Stanley
1935-1939	Don Lowe
1940	N/A

Camp Owatonna
1956	Tom Hilton
1957-1963	Phil Edwards
1964-1966	Ty Anderson
1967	Fred Beyer
1968	Verne Ullom
1969-1975	John Bower
1976	Bruce Schulze
1977-1980	Chris Cole
1981-1984	Burt Cady
1985	Bob Clark
1986-1987	Gary Crandell
1988-1989	Peter Martin
1990-1993	Seth "Chic" Johnson
1994-1996	Dave Taylor
1997-1999	Jamie Bollinger
2000-2001	Peter Martin
2002-2006	Travis Brantingham
2007-2010	Brandon Frank
2011-2012	Forrest Bless
2013-2015	Dave Pelton
2016-2021	Reid Charlston

White Feathers

Year	Senior	Junior
1957	Sterling Hamilton; David Youngblood	Jeff Hamlin; Jeff Kelly
1958	Douglas Crocker; Don Gibbs; David Purvis	Fred Martin; Don Steckler
1959	M. Barnes; Bart Jealous; Bruce Van Dyck	Fred Martin; Rick Rader
1960	Toby Cooper; Rick McCurdy	
1961	John Lyon; Fred Martin; Bruce Van Dyck	Ross Collins; Steve Parks
1962	Topper Cheatham; Dave Cook; Glenn Johnson; Terry Rodgers	Ross Collins; Jeff Moeller
1963	Topper Cheatham; Jeff Moeller; Rich Gould	
1964	Brooke Newcomb; Glenn Johnson	Harry Herrick; Tim Meyerson
1965	Steve Hayward; Glenn Johnson; Doug Potter	
1966	Jeff Moeller; Dana Wilson; Harry Herrick	Seth Johnson
1967	Jeff Moeller; Steve Bissell	Seth Johnson
1968	Scott Newsham; Seth Johnson	
1969	Mark Stevens; Ken Turkington	Peter Borden
1970	Peter Martin; Eric Beyer; Byron Shelton	Karl Zuelke
1971	Jeff Wayman; Chuck Herrick	Don MacKenzie
1972	Chuck Herrick	
1973	Colin Haynes; Scott Lambert	Doug Campbell
1974	Burke Miller	
1975	Ken Gray	
1976	Scott Eschenroeder; John Petch	
1977	Sam Snyder; Chris Dunham	Klaus Oertel
1978	Jim Lawrence	
1979	David Moore	
1980	Geoff Kelly; Fletcher Smith; Rob Estes	
1981	Claus Michelsen	
1982	John Thompson	
1983	John Thompson	

1984	John Thompson; John Dowell	
1985	John Thompson; Selby Eddy	
1986	Brad Jealous	Mike Morey
1987	Brad Jealous	
1988	Tom Greer; Todd Youngblood; Mark Rieper	
1989	Tom Greer; Mark Rieper	Dan Loomis
1990	Todd Schauman	
1991	Ryan MacGregor	
1992	Ryan MacGregor; Jon Burky	
1993	Noah Townsend	
1994	Bart Snyder	
1995	Devon Reehl; Bart Snyder	
1996	Steve Henn; Devon Reehl	
1997	Sune Tamm-Buckle; Jesse Thompson; Devon Reehl	
1998	Nick Brock; Jesse Thompson	
1999		Jeremy Robertson
2000	Spencer Holland	Duncan Wilder
2001	Jon Gregory; Spencer Holland; Jeremy Robertson; Nathan Sharp	
2002	Dana Byquist; Jordan Frank	
2003	Spencer Holland; Mitch Stock	Seth Eastman
2004	Jordan Frank	
2005	Robert Barnacle; Spencer Holland; Tyler Vane; Cameron Wells	Gibson Holland
2006	Colin Anderson; Drew Clark; Cameron Wells	
2007	Cameron Wells; Garrett Wells	
2008	Garrett Wells; Ken Stack	
2009	Garrett Wells; Gibson Holland	
2010	Ryan Richardson	
2011	Tony Bumatay; Cody Veidelis	
2012		
2013	Noel Richards	
2014		
2015	Aiden Faulstich; Cole Hoffman	
2016	Henry Howell; Henry Osborn; Boone Steele; Sean Thornton	James Osborn
2017		

2018	Austin Osborn; Dillon Hussey	
2019	Wells Faulstich; Aiden Faulstich; Joe Lake	
2020	N/A	N/A
2021	Jake Hooper; Joshua Gough	

BLACK FEATHERS

Year	Senior	Junior
1959	Bart Jealous	Buz Brewster
1960	Tom Parks; Brad Clark	Glenn Johnson; Buz Brewster
1961	Brad Clark; John Lyon; John Vernon	Glenn Johnson; Rick Rader; Gary Ullom
1962	Glenn Johnson; Rick Rader; Terry Rodgers	Andy Rohr
1963	Rich Gould	Jeff Leswing; Clark Johnson
1964	Glenn Johnson; Brooke Newcomb	Jeff Leswing
1965	Glenn Johnson; Steve Hayward	Seth Johnson
1966	Shane Kennedy	Seth Johnson
1967		Seth Johnson
1968	Seth Johnson	
1969	Seth Johnson; Jeff Wayman	
1970	Seth Johnson	Steve Turkington
1971	Jeff Wayman	Tucker Newberry
1972	Rich Coomber	Tucker Newberry; Zack Danziger
1973	Rich Coomber; Steve Willis	
1974	Burke Miller	Tucker Newberry
1975	Ken Gray	Rick Burdsall
1976	Scott Anderson	Kitt Clark; Rich Estes
1977	Mike Hastings; Sam Snyder	
1978	Scott Anderson	
1979	Scott Miller	
1980	Rob Estes	
1981	Wells Sampson	
1982		
1983	Chris "Skip" Schneider	
1984	Chris "Skip" Schneider; Dave Miller	

1985	Bryan Clark	Matt Clark
1986		Mike Morey
1987		Mike Morey; John Newland
1988	Mark Rieper	
1989	Mark Rieper; Mike Morey	
1990	Bart Spaulding	Chris Cady; Steve Coombs
1991	Mike Morey	
1992	Chris Cady	Nat Hoopes; Brian Beeman
1993	Nick Townsend	
1994		
1995		Asa Williams
1996		
1997		Spencer Holland
1998		
1999	Tyler Ragnow; Nick Brock	
2000	John Gregory; Spencer Holland	
2001	John Gregory	
2002	Spencer Holland	
2003	Steve Hart; Spencer Holland	Gabe Hoffman-Johnson
2004	Spencer Holland; Jeremy Robertson	
2005	James Suber; Gabe Hoffman-Johnson	
2006	Colin Anderson; Nick Barron; Gabe Hoffman-Johnson	Toby Howell
2007		
2008	Gabe Hoffman-Johnson	
2009		
2010		Henry Howell
2011	Tony Bumatay	
2012		Jack Schneider
2013	Henry Osborn	
2014	Henry Howell	
2015	Henry Osborn	
2016	Henry Howell; Henry Osborn	
2017	Jack Schneider	
2018		
2019	Wells Faulstich	
2020	N/A	N/A
2021		

GREENS PLAQUES

Year	Captain	Place
1957	Sterling Hamilton	2
1958	Gene Morrison	1
1959	Stephen Ross	3
1960	Toby Cooper	3
1961	Bruce Van Dyck	3
1962	Ken Lyon	3
1963	Ken Lyon	2
1964	Jim Chapman	3
1965	Andy Rodgers	3
1966	Chip Miller	2
1967	Jon Hunt	2
1968	Paul Collins	3
1969	Bruce McLane	4
1970	Peter Martin	3
1971	Steve Laver	4
1972	Steve Drake	2
1973	Steve Drake	1
1974	Peter Stevens	4
1975	Ken Gray	1
1976	Dan Newberry	3
1977	Mark Hutchinson & Mark Anderson	2
1978	Scott Anderson	2
1979	Tucker Newberry	4
1980	Rob Estes	3
1981	Stuart Barnes	4
1982	Bill Malo	1
1983	Greg Gatlin	1
1984	Selby Eddy	3
1985	Selby Eddy	1
1986	Charlie Warren	3
1987	Wally Schoenborn	3
1988	Alejo Crawford	1
1989	Andy Dickerson	2
1990	Gus Crawford	1
1991	Neil Shea	2
1992	Keith Lane	3
1993	Keith Lane	4
1994	Abenol Berhe	1
1995	Jim Prager	1
1996	Darien Day & Devon Reehl	4

1997	Devon Reehl	2
1998	John Green & Ambi Burek	4
1999	Nate Lane & Mike Vernon	3
2000	Pepy Shepard & Mark Clark	1
2001	Nate Bockley	2
2002	Tucker Savoye	2
2003	Eric Vane	2
2004	Spencer Holland	2
2005	Spencer Holland	1
2006	Colin Anderson	1
2007	Fred Toohey	1
2008	Fred Toohey	2
2009	Jordan Anderson	2
2010	Gibson Holland	1
2011	Tony Bumatay	1
2012	Nate Bermel	2
2013	Jacob Mager	3
2014	Jacquez Poole	4
2015	R. Clay Buxton	4
2016	Bryce Faulstich	2
2017	Will Towle	2
2018	Clark McFarlane	4
2019	Wells Faulstich	1
2020	N/A	N/A
2021	Carson & Hayden Oleksy	1

Place	Count
First	18
Second	19
Third	16
Fourth	11

BLUES PLAQUES

Year	Captain	Place
1957	Terry Swanson	1
1958	Pete Wilson & Pete Vernon	2
1959	Michael Barnes	1
1960	Brad Clark	2
1961	Brad Clark	1
1962	Terry Rodgers	1
1963	Terry Rodgers	1
1964	Mike McCurdy	2
1965	Glenn Johnson	1
1966	Tom Neale	1
1967	Jeff Moeller	1
1968	Scott Beyer	2
1969	Scott Moeller	2
1970	Scott Moeller	1
1971	Brad Reeves	3
1972	Erik Olsen	4
1973	Colin Haynes	2
1974	Rich Coomber	2
1975	Keith Blackmar	3
1976	Keith Blackmar	2
1977	Roger Robinson	4
1978	Dave Meyer	3
1979	Jeff Steele	2
1980	Rich Sampson	1
1981	Wells Sampson	1
1982	Brad Andrews	4
1983	Lou Sampson	2
1984	Chris "Skip" Schneider	2
1985	Dave Gillis	3
1986	Terry Coolidge	4
1987	Steve Wheeler	2
1988	Todd Youngblood	2
1989	Fred Spanjaard	3
1990	Steve Talbot	3
1991	Andre Black	1
1992	Andre Black	1
1993	Jon Burky	2
1994	Brooks Williams & Nick Vaughan	2
1995	Quinn Klinge	4
1996	Matt Vaughan	1

Year	Name	Place
1997	Seth Gregory	1
1998	Ben Vaughan	2
1999	Andrew Gorman	1
2000	Wes Gorman	3
2001	Nick Brock	1
2002	Sam Gorman	3
2003	Steve Hart	1
2004	Steve Hart	4
2005	Caleb Hoffman-Johnson	3
2006	Caleb Hoffman-Johnson	3
2007	Robert Barnacle	3
2008	Gabe Hoffman-Johnson	1
2009	Noah Sparkman	4
2010	Ryan Richardson	3
2011	Pierson Gill	3
2012	Truett Sparkman	1
2013	Tyler Winterbottom	4
2014	Sam Swoap	1
2015	Mitchell Gill	1
2016	Cole Hoffman	3
2017	Jack Schneider	1
2018	Erik Anderson	3
2019	Bo Schneider	2
2020	N/A	N/A
2021	Jake Hooper & Luca Caviness	2

Place	Count
First	23
Second	18
Third	15
Fourth	8

Reds Plaques

Year	Captain	Place
1957	David Youngblood	3
1958	Don Gibbs	3
1959	Douglas Crocker	2
1960	Tom Parks	1
1961	John Lyon	2
1962	David Cook	3
1963	Tim Bayless	3
1964	Dave Kinsman	1
1965	Doug Potter	2
1966	Bruce Cameron	3
1967	Bruce Bollinger	3
1968	Eric Beyer	4
1969	Bruce Bollinger	1
1970	Jeff Robertson	2
1971	Jeff Wayman	1
1972	Charlie Phillips	1
1973	Gair MacKenzie	3
1974	Burke Miller	1
1975	Jamie Bollinger	2
1976	Alan Boyd	4
1977	Jim MacKenzie	3
1978	Scott MacKenzie	4
1979	Scott Miller	3
1980	Andrew Abouchar	4
1981	Zack Snyder	3
1982	Zack Snyder	2
1983	Jon Dowell	4
1984	Chris Mesa	1
1985	Alan Hale	4
1986	Jay Doubman	1
1987	Erik Metzdorf	1
1988	Brad Jealous	3
1989	Chris Meyer	4
1990	Mac Spartichino	4
1991	Mike Morey	3
1992	Keith Walter	4
1993	Troy Williams	1
1994	Keith Connor	3
1995	John Tamm-Buckle	3
1996	Jason Collins	3

Year	Name	Place
1997	Noah Townsend	4
1998	Sune Tamm-Buckle	1
1999	Kramer Keller	4
2000	Andy Hatch	4
2001	Chris Evans	3
2002	Ben Waters	4
2003	Carson Krieg	4
2004	Phillip Johnson	3
2005	Andrin Foster	2
2006	Ben Bollinger	4
2007	Conrad Bollinger	2
2008	Will Smith	3
2009	Will Smith	1
2010	Conrad Bollinger	2
2011	Josh Collins	2
2012	Timmy Bollinger	4
2013	Davin Foster	2
2014	Gavin MacKenzie	3
2015	Henry Osborn	3
2016	Henry Osborn	4
2017	Austin Osborn	3
2018	Austin Osborn	1
2019	Corey Collins	4
2020	N/A	N/A
2021	Carson Miller & James Osborn	3

Place	Count
First	13
Second	11
Third	22
Fourth	18

GOLDS PLAQUES

Year	Captain	Place
1968	Pete Wagner	1
1969	Ken Turkington	3
1970	Duncan Martin	4
1971	Roger Powell	2
1972	Conrad Essen	3
1973	Mark Boutilier	4
1974	Mark Boutilier	3
1975	Darren Lepage	4
1976	Darren Lepage	1
1977	John Bullock	1
1978	Jim Herberich	1
1979	Jim Herberich	1
1980	Kitt Clark	2
1981	John Strelow	2
1982	Jon Polito	3
1983	Jeff Moore	3
1984	Greg Moore	4
1985	Bryan Clark	2
1986	Field Glover	2
1987	Rod Duret & Vlad Duret	4
1988	Vlad Duret	4
1989	Bob Whittaker	1
1990	RJ Gray	2
1991	Rich Ulm	4
1992	Stoner Glover	2
1993	Stoner Glover	3
1994	Ryan McGregor & Bart Snyder	4
1995	John Woodley	2
1996	John Woodley	2
1997	Charlie Rankin	3
1998	Charlie Ronemus & Ted Collins	3
1999	Charlie Ronemus	2
2000	Josh Reesman	2
2001	James Reed & Charlie Strickler	4
2002	Dana Byquist	1
2003	Mitch Stock	3
2004	Andy Stock	1
2005	Brad Irish	4
2006	Drew Clark	2
2007	Cameron Wells	4

Year	Name	Place
2008	Michael Scaldini	4
2009	Garrett Wells	3
2010	Alex Cowan	4
2011	Cody Veidelis	4
2012	Ian Carlson	3
2013	Gordon Strelow	1
2014	Connor D'Amico	2
2015	Denny Veidelis & Jim Masten	2
2016	Henry Howell	1
2017	Liam Peschke	4
2018	James Miles	2
2019	Braden McPhee	3
2020	N/A	N/A
2021	Ricky Lipsey & Coleman Miles	4

Place	Count
First	10
Second	15
Third	12
Fourth	16

Miscellaneous

INSPECTION SHEET (1958)

	1	2	3	4	5	6	7	8	9	10	11	12	13
Clothesline													
Cobwebs outside													
Screens													
Grounds													
Under cabin													
Wastebasket													
Floor													
Hanging clothes													
Overhead rack													
Blankets uniform													
Pajamas													
Shoes, shoelaces													
Lights off													
Shelves													
RATING													

NOTES

CAMP AREAS	CABIN	RATING
Dreamland – General Cleanup		
Dreamland – Fixtures		
Lighthouse – General Cleanup		
Lighthouse – Fixtures		
Lighthouse – Showers		
Grove – Policing, emptying cans		
Recreation Hall		
Lodge – Surrounding Grounds		
Lodge – Porch		

PLACEMENTS	SENIOR	JUNIOR
First		
Second		
Third		

Inspector: _____

PERSONALS

_____
_____
_____
_____
_____
_____
_____
_____
_____
_____
_____
_____

STAFF HANDBOOK GLOSSARY (1966)

LIGHTHOUSE:	The large bathroom and showers at the end of the grove. For the use of Braves, Warriors, & Chiefs. Counselors may use this or the counselor bath.
DREAMLAND:	Bathroom in back of the crafts shop for the use of the Scouts.
H.C.:	Head Counselor
D.L.:	Division Leader
CIT:	Counselor-in-Training. A 16 year old high school sophomore who as a camper with a partial reduction in tuition takes part in a special program of counselor training.
JUNIOR COUNSELOR:	A salaried member of the staff, who is under the age requirement of a Sr. Counselor.
BIRCHES:	Third cottage on the right when you enter camp, where the camp practitioner lives and where campers or counselors may go to rest up or recuperate when feeling under par, or just to have a chat. Counselors may use the Birches for study during their time off.
REC HALL:	Recreation Hall, used for rainy days or for weightlifting, tumbling, wrestling, and boxing. Also 2 ping pong tables.
ROCK:	The large flat rock where the camp gathers for flag ceremonies.
GROVE:	The area where all the cabins are encircled.
TEAM VILLAGES:	Each team builds a camp site, rather elaborately, in the woods on the Owatonna grounds. The Reds are on a trail off the Truck Trail down to the beach. The Blues are on a trail off the Beach Trail, and the Greens are on a trail which starts just past the Rifle Range on the way to the Boat Dock. Have a camper show you the villages.
BRIDGTON:	The nearest large town, a mile and a half by canoe across the lake, about 15 miles by car. Lots of stores and two movie theatres.
HARRISON:	The township in which we are located. The town is about a mile and a half down the road. A good

	laundromat, barbershop, and a variety store for supplies.
TRIP WEEK:	One of three weeks when everybody goes out on trips.
ZAKELO:	A Jewish Camp which neighbors us on the South and with whom we have many athletic contests.
NEWFOUND:	If you don't know what this is, you are in sad shape.
LONG LAKE LODGE:	A summer school-camp for boys from eastern prep schools who compete with us for Newfound's attention.
CHERRY ISLAND:	An island about 200 yards off the beach, owned by the camp with an A frame on it for cabin or counselor use.
NEWFOUND ISLAND:	The island off Newfound's point. We may use it with special permission from the Newfound Director.
HEADQUARTERS:	The cottage just above the grove, where the H.C. has his office, and where he and his wife live during the summer. Feel free to drop into the small living room and enter the discussion going on at the time.
COTTAGE:	The second building on the right as you enter camp, where the Director and his wife live and where the Director's office can be found.
OFFICE:	The first building on the right as you enter camp. The camp office will service your financial needs and provide you with a mimeograph machine.

DAILY SCHEDULE (1992)

MORNING

5:45am	Rise and dress (Awakened by Head Counselor)
6:00am	Wake all cabin counselors
6:15am	Second call to see that all counselors are awake
7:00am	Have bugler play reveille
7:05am	Assemble campers in the grove for "callies" and run
7:30am	Get flag from Director's Office - bring two campers from cabin to raise flag
7:35am	Ring bell for flagpole - stand in the center with Head Counselor and Directors - check for proper uniform, bring campers to attention, raise flag, and lead Pledge of Allegiance
7:45am	Lead breakfast grace - eat meal at Head Table
8:15am	Ring Inspection Bell and shout "20 minutes"
8:20am	Ring Bell and shout "15 minutes"
8:25am	Ring Bell and shout "10 minutes"
8:30am	Ring Bell and shout "5 minutes"
8:34am	Ring Bell and shout "1 minute" - count down from 10 seconds, then shout "Quiet Hour" - disqualify any cabin that is still working on Inspection
8:55am	Ring Bell for Morning Meeting - campers line up by Division in front of lodge steps and are let in by Division, youngest to oldest - post 2 counselors as ushers, one to hold lodge door and one to help seat inside
10:30am	Ring Bell to end 1st period
11:35am	Ring Bell for end of 2nd period - beginning of Free Time (Beach and Boat Dock close)
11:50am	Ring Bell and shout "Recall to Cabins"

AFTERNOON

12:00pm	Ring Bell for Lunch - campers line up by teams in front of the Lodge Porch - let team with straightest

	line in first - if buffet, stagger by divisions every 5 minutes from their cabins - Say noon grace
1:00pm	Ring Bell for Rest Hour or as soon as lunch is over - may be earlier
2:00pm	Ring Bell for end of Rest Hour - beginning of 3rd period
3:05pm	Ring Bell for end of 3rd period
4:10pm	Ring Bell for end of 4th period - beginning of Free Period
5:15pm	Beach and Boat Dock close
5:25pm	Recall to cabins
5:35pm	Ring Bell or get bugler to blow "charge" for flagpole formation - record order of cabins - announcements
5:45pm	Dinner - say dinner grace

EVENING

6:45pm	Ring Bell for Evening Activity
8:10pm	Ring Bell to end Evening Activity and shout "Scouts to the Showers" (Lighthouse)
8:30pm	Ring Bell and shout "Braves to the Showers" (Lighthouse)
8:45pm	Ring Bell and shout "Warriors to the Showers" (Lighthouse) - lights out for Scouts
9:00pm	Have bugler blow "taps" - Chiefs are quiet and complete showers (Four on the Floor)
9:15pm	Lights out for Chiefs - make sure camp is quiet, stay in grove area, check with Division Duty (DD) to make sure cabins are covered
9:30pm	Check in with Head Counselor - retire to cabin and be alert to any needs in the grove/cabin area (Counselors not on DD may leave cabin)
11:00pm	All counselors on duty retire to cabin
12:00am	Days/Nights off end

INSPECTION STANDARDS (1992)

Clothesline	No dry clothes should be on the line. All articles should be facing the same direction and uniformly arranged (i.e. towels together, wash cloths together, etc.)
Cobwebs	No cobwebs, inside or out.
Screens and Sills	Clean, free from dirt, broomstraws, etc.
Grounds	Should be free of paper, broomstraws, and litter of any kind.
Wastebasket	Empty, no puddles inside.
Hanging Clothes	Should be uniformly hung (bathrobes togethers, raincoats together, etc.) and equally spaced.
Overhead Rack	Neat, extra blankets folded, should not look like a "catch-all".
Bunks	Uniformly made, all with dustcovers the same length, all corners square, no wrinkles, no dust or straws on beds.
Trunks	Should be open and neatly arranged. No dust or sand on trunk bottom. (Counselors may leave their trunks closed).
Shoes and Laces	All shoes should be neatly lined up with laces untied and tucked in.
Shutters	Should be free of dust and dirt with nothing behind them.
Shelves	Should be neat and orderly, free from dust and dirt.
Lights	Off at the time of inspection.
Floor	Free of dirt and dust balls.

TRIPLE CROWN WINNERS

- Terry Rodgers (Blues '62)
- Glenn Johnson (Blues '65)
- Jeff Wayman (Reds '71)
- Burke Miller (Reds '74)
- Ken Gray (Greens '75)
- Colin Anderson (Greens '06)
- Tony Bumatay (Greens '11)
- Henry Howell (Golds '16)
- Wells Faulstich (Greens '19)

Acknowledgements

This book was made possible by the contributions of many alumni who were more than happy to share stories and photos of their time at Camp. Of course, I wanted to speak to so many more of you; those I was able to speak to are listed on the next page.

A few people went above and beyond in their support of this project. First, Phoebe "Pemy" MacKenzie Smith was essential—without the boxes of documents and photos that belonged to her grandfather Frank Hayden Connor and other family members, this book wouldn't be half of what it is. Phoebe was also incredibly supportive by opening her home to me and letting me turn her dining room into a research basecamp.

Additional support came from longtime friends of Camp, including Jamie Bollinger, Sara Osborn, Glenn Johnson, Rich Coomber, and my C.I.T. counselor Mike Vernon, who all provided edits and feedback on various drafts of the book. Anne Wold was a ready resource when I had questions about the early years. Jenny Green and Andrew Parsons helped saved the day when it came to finding photos to use. My Cabin 4 counselor Evan MacDonald dug through his storage and found a bin of great materials, which he then drove all the way to Maine for me to pick up. Thanks to you all!

Interviews conducted by phone and email:

Terry Batty	July 2020
Eric Beyer	May 2021
Forrest Bless	June 2021
Jamie Bollinger	May 2021
Travis Brantingham	May 2021
Burt Cady	March 2021
Reid Charlston	May 2021
David Cook	August 2020
Rich Coomber	September 2020
Gary Crandell	June 2020
Brandon Frank	June 2021
Nolen Harter	July 2020
Seth "Chic" Johnson	May 2021
Evan MacDonald	May 2021
Marcia Martin	May 2021
Scott Moeller	November 2020
Erik Olsen	May 2021
Dave Pelton	May 2021
Bill Rupp	September 2020
Weldon Rutledge	December 2020
Wells Sampson	October 2020
Kim Schuette	June 2021
Don Steckler	September 2020
Phil "Flip" Steckler	August 2020
David Taylor	February 2021
Mike Vernon	July 2021
Peter Weaver	December 2020
Duncan Wilder	June 2020
Anne Wold	August 2019
David Youngblood	September 2020

ENDNOTES

[1] Echo Newsletter, Vol. 2, No. 4, 1958, Phoebe (Pemy) MacKenzie Smith Collection; Sally Romero Manley reminiscence, ca 1996, Camp Owatonna Archive.

[2] Hal Heim reminiscence, 1997, Camp Owatonna Archive; Sally Romero Manley reminiscence.

[3] Sally Romero Manley reminiscence.

[4] *Bicentennial History of Harrison, Maine, 1905-2005* (Harrison, ME: Penobscot Press, 2005), 250; Echo Newsletter, Vol. 2, No. 4; Letter from Frank H. Connor to L.R. Ringhofer, July 9, 1975, Phoebe (Pemy) MacKenzie Smith Collection.

[5] Letter from Frank H. Connor to L.R. Ringhofer.

[6] Echo Newsletter, August 1934, Camp Owatonna Archive.

[7] Newfound/Owatonna Newsletter, Winter 2000, Phoebe (Pemy) MacKenzie Smith Collection.

[8] Newfound/Owatonna Newsletter, May 1996, Phoebe (Pemy) MacKenzie Smith Collection; Letter from Frank H. Connor to L.R. Ringhofer.

[9] Census: George Stanley, 1900, Ancestry.com; Census: George Stanley, 1905, Ancestry.com; Census: George Stanley, 1915, Ancestry.com.

[10] U.S. Census: George Stanley, 1900; U.S. Census: George Stanley, 1930, Ancestry.com.

[11] Letter from Frank H. Connor to L.R. Ringhofer.

[12] U.S. Census: George Stanley, 1905.

[13] Ida Eltringham, n.d., Ancestry.com.

[14] Marriage Record: George and Gertrude Stanley, 1914, Ancestry.com.

15 Tessa Anable Bollinger, *100 Years at Camp Newfound, 1914-2013* (Portland, ME: Curry Printing Company, 2013).

16 Bollinger. Gertrude is seen in the 1917 all-camp photo for Newfound.

17 U.S. Census: George Stanley, 1915.

18 *Centennial History of Harrison, Maine* (Portland, ME: Southworth Printing Company, 1909).

19 *Centennial History of Harrison, Maine*.

20 "Joseph Chaplin Attends Horse Trot," *Bridgton News*, March 7, 1919.

21 Deed: Luther C. Edwards to Joseph Chaplin, November 6, 1908, Cumberland County Registry of Deeds.

22 Records from the Cumberland County Registry of Deeds indicate the property lineage includes: Stephen W. Blake to John B. Sanderson (1868), to Asa P. Whitney (1869), to Marietta M. Kneeland (1883), to Albert S. Kneeland (1891), to Luther C. Edwards (1905), to Joseph S. Chaplin (1908), to George A. Stanley (1920). An 1857 map of Harrison confirms Stephen Blake resided on the property, and an 1871 map confirms that Asa P. Whitney resided on the property, and that his neighbor occupying Bluff Point—what is today Camp Newfound—was George H. Kneeland, a relative by marriage. See 1857 Map of Cumberland County in the Library of Congress online archives; *Centennial History of Harrison, Maine*; 1871 Map of Harrison; *Bicentennial History of Harrison, Maine*, 42.

23 Deed: Joseph Chaplin to George Stanley, March 26, 1920, Cumberland County Registry of Deeds.

24 Deed: Joseph Chaplin to Charles E. Roberts, March 29, 1911, Cumberland County Registry of Deeds.

25 Joseph Chaplin timeline, 1859-1931, July 4, 1931, Ancestry.com.

26 The purchase of Ropioa occurred soon after World War I, which ended in November 1918. Local resident Archie Belanger believes that the U.S. Army Corps of Engineers used the property to train lifeboat and ambulance

crews, and that they built barracks and a mess hall, i.e. the Lodge, there. The author's research was unable to verify this information.

[27] Deed: Joseph Chaplin to George Stanley.

[28] "Joseph S. Chaplin Sold Farm," *Bridgton News*, April 2, 1920.

[29] U.S. Census: Joseph Chaplin, 1920, Ancestry.com; "Joseph S. Chaplin Dead," *The Lewiston Daily Sun*, July 6, 1931.

[30] "George Stanley Selling Horses," *Bridgton News*, August 20, 1920.

[31] "Cook Wanted," *Bridgton News*, March 18, 1921; "Young Ladies Wanted," *Bridgton News*, June 24, 1921.

[32] An advertisement for Camp Ropioa in an April 20, 1941, issue of the *New York Herald Tribune* notes that the camp is in its 19th year, verifying that it started in 1922. The 1935 edition of *A Handbook of Summer Camps* records that Camp Ropioa was established in 1922.

[33] "Camp Ropioa," *Christian Science Monitor*, June 1, 1922.

[34] Photo: All-camp photo, Kahill Photo Studios, Portland, ME, 2R112, 1922, Camp Owatonna Archive.

[35] Hal Heim's reminiscence says the color of the Ropioa uniform was blue.

[36] Photo: Ropioa Lodge and flagpole, Kahill Photo Studios, Portland, ME, 2R52, 1922, Camp Owatonna Archive; Photo: Camp Ropioa panorama, Kahill Photo Studios, Portland, ME, 2R11, 1922, Camp Owatonna Archive.

[37] Newfound/Owatonna Newsletter, May 1996.

[38] P.E. Sargent, *A Handbook of American Private Schools*, vol. 8, 1923.

[39] Gertrude Stanley to Frank H. Connor, September 6, 1923, Phoebe (Pemy) MacKenzie Smith Collection.

[40] Gertrude Stanley to Frank H. Connor.

[41] Photo: All-camp photo, Kahill Photo Studios, Portland, ME, 5R63, 1925, Camp Owatonna Archive; Photo: Ropioa Lodge and tents, Kahill Photo Studios, Portland, ME, 5R13, 1925, Camp Owatonna Archive.

[42] Photo: All-camp photo, Kahill Photo Studio, Portland, ME, 5R62, 1925, Phoebe (Pemy) MacKenzie Smith Collection; Photo: All-camp photo, Kahill Photo Studios, Portland, ME, 5R63.

[43] Photo: All-camp photo, Kahill Photo Studio, Portland, ME, 5R62, 1925, Phoebe (Pemy) MacKenzie Smith Collection; Photo: Mr. Stanley with campers in Lodge, Kahill Photo Studios, Portland, ME, 5R63, 1925, Phoebe (Pemy) MacKenzie Smith Collection.

[44] Photo: Camp Ropioa, Kahill-Spratt Photo Studios, 8RP12, 1928, Camp Owatonna Archive; Author's interview with Bill Rupp, September 3, 2020.

[45] Photo: Ropioa P.G.T. meeting, Kahill-Spratt Photo Studios, Portland, ME, 8RP63, 1928, Phoebe (Pemy) MacKenzie Smith Collection.

[46] Charlotte Weisenberg, "Maine's Summer Camps for Jewish Youth in the Mid-Twentieth Century", academic paper, Colby College, Spring 2013, https://web.colby.edu/jewsinmaine/maine/summer-camps/.

[47] Photo: Sunday School in the Lodge, Kahill-Spratt Photo Studios, Portland, ME, 8RP61, 1928, Phoebe (Pemy) MacKenzie Smith Collection; Photo: Sunday School in the Lodge, Kahill-Spratt Photo Studios, Portland, ME, 8RP62, 1928, Phoebe (Pemy) MacKenzie Smith Collection.

[48] Photo: All-camp photo, Kahill-Spratt Photo Studios, 8RP11, 1928, Camp Owatonna Archive.

[49] Photo: All-camp photo, Kahill Photo Studios, Portland, ME, 9rp11, 1929, Camp Owatonna Archive.

[50] Cabin photo from John M. Weil, 1929, Camp Owatonna Archive.

[51] Echo Newsletter, August 1934.

[52] Directory of Bridgton, Casco, Harrison, Naples and Raymond, 1930 1929.

[53] Hal Heim reminiscence.

[54] Hal Heim reminiscence.

[55] Hal Heim reminiscence.

56 Echo Newsletter, July 19, 1934, Camp Owatonna Archive.

57 Echo Newsletter, July 4, 1934, Camp Owatonna Archive.

58 Echo Newsletter, August 1, 1934, Camp Owatonna Archive.

59 Hal Heim reminiscence.

60 Echo Newsletter, August 21, 1934, Camp Owatonna Archive.

61 Echo Newsletter, July 14, 1934, Camp Owatonna Archive.

62 Echo Newsletter.

63 Echo Newsletter, July 13, 1934, 13, Camp Owatonna Archive.

64 Hal Heim reminiscence.

65 "Lucy Nicolar Goes Far From a Maine Indian Reservation — And Then Returns," New England Historical Society, 2020, https://www.newenglandhistoricalsociety.com/lucy-nicolar-uplifts-people/.

66 Echo Newsletter, July 28, 1934, Camp Owatonna Archive.

67 Echo Newsletter, August 1934.

68 Echo Newsletter, August 24, 1934, Camp Owatonna Archive.

69 Newfound/Owatonna Newsletter, May 1996; Letter from Frank H. Connor to L.R. Ringhofer; Memory book, Camp Newfound, 1955, Phoebe (Pemy) MacKenzie Smith Collection; Letter from Owatonna Board of Trustees, November 1957, Phoebe (Pemy) MacKenzie Smith Collection.

70 Deed: George Stanley to the Lowes, August 28, 1935, Cumberland County Registry of Deeds; "Sold to Don Lowe," *Bridgton News*, September 20, 1935.

71 Birth Record: Don Lowe, December 15, 1903, Ancestry.com; Seventieth Annual Report of the Town of Swampscott, Mass., 1921.

72 The Paean Yearbook, Phillips Exeter Academy, 1923, 72.

73 "Donald S. Lowe," *Christian Science Monitor*, December 10, 1932.

74 "Enid Goss Marriage Announcement," *Ontario Ladies College*, June 1933. A wedding gift they received was a painting from famed Canadian

ornithologist and painter Doris Heustis Mills Speirs, who was also a Christian Scientist. Later, Enid published several poems in the *Christian Science Monitor*.

75 "Camp Ropioa," *Christian Science Monitor*, July 2, 1936.

76 "Sold to Don Lowe."

77 Hal Heim reminiscence.

78 Bollinger, *100 Years at Camp Newfound, 1914-2013*, 302.

79 Bollinger, 190.

80 Bollinger, 284.

81 Deed: The Lowes to George Stanley, December 28, 1939, Cumberland County Registry of Deeds.

82 Don Lowe's draft card, 1942, Ancestry.com.

83 Don and Enid Lowe voter registrations, 1944, Ancestry.com; Directory: Don and Enid Lowe, 1951, Ancestry.com.

84 Anne Wold's interview with William "Bill" Connelly, August 11, 2010.

85 Author's interview with Bill Rupp.

86 Letter from Frank H. Connor to L.R. Ringhofer.

87 Sally Romero Manley reminiscence.

88 Lien: George Stanley, January 11, 1944, Cumberland County Registry of Deeds.

89 Death Record: George Stanley, February 16, 1947, Town Records of Niantic, CT.

90 Letter from Gertrude Stanley to Phil Edwards, August 12, 1958, Phoebe (Pemy) MacKenzie Smith Collection.

91 Death Record: Gertrude Stanley, Connecticut Death Records Index, July 20, 1960.

92 Ropioa Review Newsletter, Vol. 14, 1954, Camp Owatonna Archive; "Camp Ropioa 19th Year," *New York Herald Tribune*, April 20, 1941.

93 Author's interview with Anne Wold, 2020.

94 Ropioa Review Newsletter, Vol. 14.

95 Bollinger, *100 Years at Camp Newfound, 1914-2013*.

96 Deed: LaMarsh and DeMascola, March 7, 1952, Cumberland County Registry of Deeds.

97 "Camps Ropioa and Tawasi," *Chappaqua Sunday*, April 28, 1955, https://nyshistoricnewspapers.org/lccn/sn2001062038/1955-04-28/ed-1/seq-7/; *Bicentennial History of Harrison, Maine, 1905-2005*, 2005, 251.

98 Henry Johnson, "Camp Zakelo & Long Lake Lodge" (Maine Summer Camp News, Winter 2019), https://mainecamps.org/content/uploads/2019/01/Winter-2019-Newsletter.pdf.

99 "Camp Passaconaway Choir Boys," *Daily Boston Globe*, July 6, 1929; "Camp Passaconaway," *New York Herald Tribune*, June 11, 1939, 11; "Sumner Stone Auction, Waterford, ca. 1910," Maine Memory Network, 2013, https://www.mainememory.net/artifact/81041.

100 "Camp Passaconaway," *Christian Science Monitor*, July 8, 1933.

101 "Camp Passaconaway," *Washington Post*, May 16, 1943; List of Christian Science boys at Camp Passaconaway, 1948, Phoebe (Pemy) MacKenzie Smith Collection.

102 "Camp Passaconaway," *Christian Science Monitor*, April 10, 1954; "Camp Passaconaway," *New York Herald Tribune*, May 8, 1955.

103 List of Christian Science boys at Camp Passaconaway, 1953, Phoebe (Pemy) MacKenzie Smith Collection.

104 Email from David Youngblood, September 15, 2020.

105 Email from David Youngblood.

106 "Sumner Stone Auction, Waterford, ca. 1910."

[107] "Ropioa Cabins Burn," *Bridgton News*, August 27, 1948; *Bicentennial History of Harrison, Maine, 1905-2005*, vol. 2 (Harrison, ME: Penobscot Press, 2005), 92.

[108] Deed: Stanley and LaMarsh, February 9, 1952, Cumberland County Registry of Deeds; Lawsuit discharged: John LaMarsh, February 28, 1952, Cumberland County Registry of Deeds; Deed: Morris and LaMarsh, March 10, 1952, Cumberland County Registry of Deeds; Deed: C. Pappas and Ropioa, February 28, 1952, Cumberland County Registry of Deeds.

[109] See records for John and Irene LaMarsh in the Cumberland County Registry of Deeds.

[110] Deed: LaMarsh and DeMascola.

[111] "Foreclosure on John LaMarsh," September 30, 1954, Cumberland County Registry of Deeds.

[112] Echo Newsletter, August 17, 1963, Phoebe (Pemy) MacKenzie Smith Collection; Echo Newsletter, Vol. 2, No. 4.

[113] Timeline of Carl Fischer, Inc., 1999, http://www.brasshistory.net/Fischer%20History.pdf.

[114] Letter from Frank H. Connor to L.R. Ringhofer.

[115] Correspondence between Dorothy H. Cobb and Phoebe Connor, August 5, 1955, Phoebe (Pemy) MacKenzie Smith Collection.

[116] Newfound Camp for Boys Association, State of Maine Certificate of Organization, November 4, 1955, Camp Owatonna Archive.

[117] Deed: Benjamin A. DeMascola to Newfound Camp for Boys Association, January 4, 1956, Cumberland County Registry of Deeds.

[118] Correspondence between Dorothy H. Cobb and Phoebe Connor, August 5, 1955.

[119] Lists of Christian Science boys at Camp Passaconaway, 1948, '53, '54, '55, Phoebe MacKenzie Smith Collection.

[120] Letter from Frank H. Connor, November 1955, Phoebe (Pemy) MacKenzie Smith Collection.

[121] "Camp Ropioa," *Christian Science Monitor,* December 3, 1955. Note, the date of 1938 is likely inaccurate.

[122] Letter from Phoebe Connor, November 1955, Phoebe (Pemy) MacKenzie Smith Collection; Letter from Dorothy H. Cobb to Phoebe Connor, January 18, 1956, Phoebe (Pemy) MacKenzie Smith Collection; Correspondence between Dorothy H. Cobb and Phoebe Connor, February 1956, Phoebe (Pemy) MacKenzie Smith Collection; Letter from Dorothy H. Cobb to Phoebe Connor, April 15, 1956, Phoebe (Pemy) MacKenzie Smith Collection.

[123] Letter from Dorothy H. Cobb to Phoebe Ann Connor, February 24, 1956, Phoebe (Pemy) MacKenzie Smith Collection.

[124] Author's interview with Weldon Rutledge, December 11, 2020.

[125] "Tom Hilton," *Traverse City Record Eagle,* January 9, 1988.

[126] "John LaMarsh Vacationing in Bridgeport," *The Bridgeport Post,* July 9, 1958; Deed: Jackson and LaMarsh, February 15, 1958, Cumberland County Registry of Deeds.

[127] Letter from Dorothy H. Cobb, 1956, Phoebe (Pemy) MacKenzie Smith Collection; Letter from Frank H. Connor to L.R. Ringhofer; Letter from Tom Hilton to parents, 1956, Phoebe (Pemy) MacKenzie Smith Collection; Correspondence between Dorothy H. Cobb and Phoebe Connor, May 1956, Phoebe (Pemy) MacKenzie Smith Collection.

[128] Letter from Frank H. Connor to L.R. Ringhofer.

[129] Letter from Tom Hilton to parents.

[130] Letter from Frank H. Connor to L.R. Ringhofer.

[131] Pamphlet, Newfound Camp for Boys, Inc., 1956, Phoebe (Pemy) MacKenzie Smith Collection; Document listing scholarships awarded, 1956, Phoebe (Pemy) MacKenzie Smith Collection.

[132] Pamphlet, Newfound Camp for Boys, Inc.

[133] Weisenberg, Maine's Summer Camps for Jewish Youth.

[134] Newfound/Owatonna Newsletter, Winter 2000.

¹³⁵ Author's interview with Weldon Rutledge. When Leelanau started in the early 1920s, it featured two teams. From the late 1920s through the mid 1970s, it had the three teams. In 1974, it switched again to two teams, North and South, out of necessity because its enrollment shrunk after its decision to only allow Christian Science campers to attend. Its use of Indian lore seemed to decline during the 1960s and 1970s, and it seems to have been completely dropped by the late 1980s.

¹³⁶ Newfound/Owatonna Newsletter, Winter 2000. David Youngblood recalls that the teams were formed his second year, when he was a C.I.T., in 1957. This would explain why the plaques begin in 1957. However, Phil Edwards, whose first year as director was in 1957, attributes the creation of the teams to Tom Hilton in 1956. So, Hilton may have created the teams in 1956, but the team competition may have been created in 1957 by Edwards.

¹³⁷ William Oliver Bright, *Native American Placenames of the United States* (Norman, OK: University of Oklahoma Press, 2004), 436.

¹³⁸ Bright, 378.

¹³⁹ Geoffrey Parkinson, "Abenaki," in *The Gale Encyclopedia of Native American Tribes* (Detroit, MI: Gale, 1998), 9–10.

¹⁴⁰ Ed Decker, "Penobscot," in *The Gale Encyclopedia of Native American Tribes* (Detroit, MI: Gale, 2004), 234.

¹⁴¹ Bright, *Native American Placenames of the United States*, 378.

¹⁴² Decker, "Penobscot," 234–35.

¹⁴³ Lists of Owatonna campers, ca 1957, Phoebe (Pemy) MacKenzie Smith Collection.

¹⁴⁴ Email from David Youngblood.

¹⁴⁵ Email from David Youngblood.

¹⁴⁶ Email from David Youngblood.

¹⁴⁷ Email from David Youngblood.

¹⁴⁸ Letter from Owatonna Board of Trustees.

[149] "Tom Hilton."

[150] Author's interview with Weldon Rutledge.

[151] Echo Newsletter, August 21, 1965, Phoebe (Pemy) MacKenzie Smith Collection.

[152] Newfound/Owatonna Newsletter, Winter 2000.

[153] "Principia Athletics Hall of Fame: Phil Edwards," 2010, http://www.principiaalumni.org/halloffame/edwards; The Blade Yearbook, Principia Upper School, 1965. Bole captained the varsity rugby team at Cambridge University, and he also represented England in a series of post-war rugby matches. Bole is the author of the Christian Science article "Be the Best," which is popular with Owatonna counselors. See J. R. Suber, *Be the Best: The Rugby Career of Eric Bole* (Amazon, 2020).

[154] Email from David Youngblood.

[155] See Edwards's article in the Newfound/Owatonna newsletter from Winter 2000.

[156] Echo Newsletter, August 17, 1957, Phoebe (Pemy) MacKenzie Smith Collection.

[157] Email from David Youngblood.

[158] Echo Newsletter, Vol. 2, No. 4.

[159] Email from David Youngblood. Youngblood says Edwards created it in 1957.

[160] Echo Newsletter, August 17, 1957.

[161] Echo Newsletter.

[162] Letter from Phil Edwards to parents, August 21, 1957, Phoebe (Pemy) MacKenzie Smith Collection.

[163] Email from David Youngblood.

[164] Echo Newsletter, August 17, 1957.

[165] Echo Newsletter.

[166] Author's interview with Jamie Bollinger, May 25, 2021.

[167] Letter from Phil Edwards to parents, August 21, 1957.

[168] Letter from Phil Edwards to campers, June 1957, Phoebe (Pemy) MacKenzie Smith Collection.

[169] List of Owatonna campers, 1957, Phoebe (Pemy) MacKenzie Smith Collection.

[170] Letter from Howard Galloway to Frank H. Connor, November 19, 1957, Phoebe (Pemy) MacKenzie Smith Collection.

[171] Echo Newsletter, August 17, 1957.

[172] Echo Newsletter.

[173] Letter from Bill Bodine to Frank H. Connor, July 8, 1958, Phoebe (Pemy) MacKenzie Smith Collection.

[174] Letter from Phil Edwards to parents, August 18, 1958, Phoebe (Pemy) MacKenzie Smith Collection.

[175] Letter from Phil Edwards to Frank H. Connor, June 28, 1958, Phoebe (Pemy) MacKenzie Smith Collection.

[176] Letter from Phil Edwards to parents, August 18, 1958.

[177] Echo Newsletter, July 22, 1958, Phoebe (Pemy) MacKenzie Smith Collection.

[178] Letter from Bill Bodine to Frank H. Connor.

[179] Letter from Bill Bodine to Frank H. Connor.

[180] Echo Newsletter, Vol. 2, No. 4.

[181] Letter from Phil Edwards to parents, July 21, 1958, Phoebe (Pemy) MacKenzie Smith Collection.

[182] Echo Newsletter, July 22, 1958.

[183] Owatonna record books, 1957-1967, Evan MacDonald Collection.

[184] Newfound/Owatonna Newsletter, Winter 2000.

[185] Echo Newsletter, Vol. 2, No. 3, 1958, 3, Phoebe (Pemy) MacKenzie Smith Collection.

[186] Echo Newsletter, Vol. 2, No. 4.

[187] Echo Newsletter, Vol. 2, No. 4.

[188] Echo Newsletter, Vol. 2, No. 4.

[189] Echo Newsletter, 1959, Phoebe (Pemy) MacKenzie Smith Collection.

[190] Echo Newsletter. Jealous went on to graduate from the U.S. Naval Academy, then became a Marine Corps helicopter pilot in Vietnam and later flew missions for the CIA's Air America in Laos. Brewster went on to set football and basketball records at Principia College, and in 1969 was briefly signed but ultimately cut from Vince Lombardi's Washington Redskins.

[191] Meeting notes, Board of Trustees, August 20, 1960, Phoebe (Pemy) MacKenzie Smith Collection.

[192] Meeting notes, Board of Trustees, August 21, 1959, Phoebe (Pemy) MacKenzie Smith Collection.

[193] This change is visible on the Inspection plaques in the Lodge.

[194] Letter from Boyd N. Jones to parents, April 23, 1957, Phoebe (Pemy) MacKenzie Smith Collection.

[195] Meeting notes, Board of Trustees, August 20, 1961, Phoebe (Pemy) MacKenzie Smith Collection.

[196] Letter from Phil Edwards to Frank H. Connor and Phoebe F. Connor, February 9, 1958, Phoebe (Pemy) MacKenzie Smith Collection.

[197] "Doc Singer Dead," *Bridgton News*, May 5, 1966.

[198] Meeting notes, Board of Trustees, August 20, 1961.

[199] Letter from Phil Edwards to parents, July 21, 1958, 21; Deed: Leona E. Roberts and Owatonna Camp for Boys Association, July 20, 1963, Cumberland County Registry of Deeds.

[200] Sally Romero Manley reminiscence.

201 Letter from Phil Edwards to Gordon MacRae, August 5, 1959, Phoebe (Pemy) MacKenzie Smith Collection.

202 Letter from Boyd N. Jones to parents.

203 Letter from Frank H. Connor, August 2, 1961, Phoebe (Pemy) MacKenzie Smith Collection.

204 Meeting notes, Board of Trustees, August 20, 1960; "Camp Owatonna," *Christian Science Monitor*, March 11, 1961.

205 Newfound/Owatonna Newsletter, Winter 2000.

206 Owatonna record books.

207 Letter from Frank H. Connor to Phil Edwards, October 20, 1961, Phoebe (Pemy) MacKenzie Smith Collection; Echo Newsletter, August 6, 1963, Phoebe (Pemy) MacKenzie Smith Collection.

208 Bollinger, *100 Years at Camp Newfound, 1914-2013*.

209 Meeting notes, Board of Trustees, June 17, 1961, Phoebe (Pemy) MacKenzie Smith Collection; Meeting notes, Board of Trustees, August 20, 1961; Bollinger, *100 Years at Camp Newfound, 1914-2013*.

210 Echo Newsletter, August 17, 1963.

211 Camp Owatonna pamphlet, 1968, Phoebe (Pemy) MacKenzie Smith Collection.

212 "USTA Hall of Fame: Phil Edwards," 1996, https://www.usta.com/content/dam/usta/sections/missouri-valley/pdfs/HoF_History.pdf; "Principia Athletics Hall of Fame: Phil Edwards."

213 "Principia Athletics Hall of Fame: Thiers 'Ty' Anderson," Principia Alumni, 2014, http://www.principiaalumni.org/halloffame/anderson.

214 Owatonna Staff Handbook, 1966, Evan MacDonald Collection.

215 Author's interview with Terry Batty, July 14, 2020.

216 Owatonna Staff Handbook.

217 Echo Newsletter, August 21, 1965.

218 Bollinger, *100 Years at Camp Newfound, 1914-2013*; Echo Newsletter, August 21, 1965; Glenn Johnson awards, 1965, Camp Owatonna Archive.

219 Echo Newsletter, August 20, 1966, Phoebe (Pemy) MacKenzie Smith Collection; Echo Newsletter, August 21, 1964, Phoebe (Pemy) MacKenzie Smith Collection.

220 Echo Newsletter, August 21, 1964.

221 Echo Newsletter.

222 Echo Newsletter.

223 Echo Newsletter.

224 Echo Newsletter, August 21, 1965.

225 Email from Scott Moeller, February 2, 2021.

226 Deed: DeMascola and Owatonna, September 9, 1965, Cumberland County Registry of Deeds.

227 Meeting notes, Board of Trustees, August 22, 1964, Phoebe (Pemy) MacKenzie Smith Collection; Bollinger, *100 Years at Camp Newfound, 1914-2013*.

228 Echo Newsletter, August 20, 1966.

229 Echo Newsletter, August 21, 1965.

230 Echo Newsletter.

231 Camp Owatonna pamphlet.

232 "Principia Athletics Hall of Fame: Thiers 'Ty' Anderson."

233 Echo Newsletter, August 20, 1966.

234 Author's interview with Jamie Bollinger.

235 Author's interview with Eric Beyer, May 29, 2021; Kim M. Schuette, *Christian Science Military Ministry, 1917-2004* (Indianapolis, Indiana: Brockton

Publishing Company, 2008); Author's interview with Kim Schuette, June 2021.

[236] Author's interview with Erik Olsen, May 24, 2021.

[237] Camp Newfound/Owatonna Newsletter, February 1997, Phoebe (Pemy) MacKenzie Smith Collection.

[238] Author's interview with Jamie Bollinger; Author's interview with Eric Beyer.

[239] Although different from the pump used for the Beyer-era waterslide, the remnants of an old car engine can still be found in the lake, adjacent to the concrete steps between the Boat Dock and Newfound. It is believed this old pump was once used to bring water from the lake up to the Lodge.

[240] Author's interview with Nolen Harter, July 6, 2020; Author's interview with Eric Beyer; Author's interview with Jamie Bollinger.

[241] Author's interview with Eric Beyer.

[242] Author's interview with Jamie Bollinger.

[243] Author's interview with Nolen Harter.

[244] Author's interview with Nolen Harter.

[245] Author's interviews with Jamie Bollinger and Scott Moeller.

[246] Author's interview with Burt Cady, March 28, 2021.

[247] "Brooklyn Tigers Sign Grid Star," *Christian Science Monitor*, July 12, 1944.

[248] "Bates' Verne Ullom To Coach Principia," *Associated Press*, April 23, 1958; "Coach Switches Jobs," *Washington Post*, May 14, 1963.

[249] Letter from Verne Ullom to Frank and Phoebe Connor, January 8, 1968, Phoebe (Pemy) MacKenzie Smith Collection.

[250] Laurie Collier Hillstrom, "Lakota," in *The Gale Encyclopedia of Native American Tribes* (Detroit, MI: Gale, 1998), 288.

[251] Hillstrom, 296.

252 Letter from Frank H. Connor to Verne Ullom, January 11, 1969, Phoebe (Pemy) MacKenzie Smith Collection.

253 "Hall of Fame: John Bower," Middlebury Athletics, 2014, https://athletics.middlebury.edu/honors/hall-of-fame/john-bower/1; "John Bower," Wikipedia, n.d., https://en.wikipedia.org/wiki/John_Bower; Lisa Lynn, "RIP John Bower: Nordic Legend and Middlebury Coach," *VT Ski & Ride*, June 8, 2017, https://vtskiandride.com/rip-john-bower-nordic-legend-middlebury-coach/; Ross Atkin, "In a Land Where Skiing Is Sports The US Once Claimed Victory," *Christian Science Monitor*, February 3, 1994, https://www.csmonitor.com/1994/0203/03121.html.

254 Letter from Frank H. Connor to L.R. Ringhofer.

255 John Bower, "An Interview: With a Champion Skier," *Christian Science Sentinel*, November 1, 1969, https://sentinel.christianscience.com/issues/1969/11/71-44/an-interview-with-a-champion-skier; Elizabeth F. Bower, Robert Bower, and John F. Bower, "Testimony of Healing," *Christian Science Sentinel*, August 5, 1972, https://sentinel.christianscience.com/issues/1972/8/74-32/for-over-thirty-years-our-family-has-received-great-blessings-as-a; John Bower, "Right Motives for Skiing," *Christian Science Sentinel*, February 21, 2014, https://sentinel.christianscience.com/web-originals/2014/right-motives-for-skiing.

256 Author's interview with Seth Johnson, May 25, 2021.

257 Author's interview with Gary Crandell, June 22, 2020.

258 Author's interview with Jamie Bollinger.

259 Letter from Seth F. Johnson to parents, October 1968, Phoebe (Pemy) MacKenzie Smith Collection.

260 Bollinger, *100 Years at Camp Newfound, 1914-2013*, 310.

261 Bollinger, 282.

262 Bollinger, 219.

263 Author's interview with Rich Coomber, September 3, 2020.

264 It is not known when the idea of the "Triple Crown" came to be, perhaps by the early 2000s. Interestingly, records as early as 1959 refer to "Grand Slam Winners" as those who won a combination of feathers and team competition; see Owatonna record books, 1957-1967, Evan MacDonald Collection.

265 Newfound/Owatonna Newsletter, Winter 2000.

266 Newfound/Owatonna Newsletter.

267 Author's interview with Erik Olsen.

268 Bollinger, *100 Years at Camp Newfound, 1914-2013*, 17.

269 Bollinger, 17.

270 Pack 'N Paddle flyer, 1973, Phoebe (Pemy) MacKenzie Smith Collection.

271 Author's interview with Seth and Glenn Johnson.

272 Owatonna Staff Handbook.

273 Meeting notes, Board of Trustees, September 22, 1968, Phoebe (Pemy) MacKenzie Smith Collection.

274 Owatonna Staff List, 1973, Evan MacDonald Collection.

275 Author's interview with Rich Coomber.

276 "History, 1868-2010," American Camp Association, n.d., http://www.acacamp.org/anniversary/timeline/.

277 Bollinger, *100 Years at Camp Newfound, 1914-2013*; BJ Phillips, "Summer Camps: How Safe?," *Washington Post*, April 27, 1969; "Decisions on Summer Camp Safety," *Washington Post*, February 5, 1975.

278 Letter from Frank H. Connor to L.R. Ringhofer.

279 "Hall of Fame: John Bower"; "John Bower"; Tom Kelly, "Olympian and Coach John Bower Passes," US Ski & Snowboard, June 8, 2017, https://usskiandsnowboard.org/news/olympian-and-coach-john-bower-passes.

280 Brandon Frank, "Putting on the 'New Man,'" *Call of the Loon*, Spring 2008, Evan MacDonald Collection.

281 Letter from Warren G. MacKenzie to parents, December 15, 1975, Phoebe (Pemy) MacKenzie Smith Collection; "Springfield College Bulletin," October 1973, 26.

282 Meeting notes, Board of Trustees, July 31, 1976, Phoebe (Pemy) MacKenzie Smith Collection.

283 Email from Wells Sampson, October 2, 2020.

284 "James Herberich," Olympics Athlete Profile, n.d., https://olympics.com/en/athletes/james-herberich.

285 "Paul Christian Cole," *Tulsa World*, March 30, 1999, https://tulsaworld.com/archive/obituaries/article_83f20850-af98-5abc-b1f6-a42bb291c1b5.html; Christian Cole, 40th Annual Star Island Conference, Institute on Religion in an Age of Science, August 1993, https://www.iras.org/uploads/1/7/5/4/17545549/conference_book_1993.pdf.

286 Author's interview with Jamie Bollinger.

287 Letter from Chris Cole to staff, Spring 1978, Phoebe (Pemy) MacKenzie Smith Collection.

288 "Free Soccer Clinic," *Christian Science Monitor*, June 2, 1980; "Camp Owatonna," *Christian Science Monitor*, May 5, 1980.

289 Author's interview with Seth Johnson.

290 Trip Reports, Summer 1977, Phoebe (Pemy) MacKenzie Smith Collection.

291 Newfound/Owatonna Newsletter, April 15, 1977, Phoebe (Pemy) MacKenzie Smith Collection.

292 Author's interview with Jamie Bollinger.

293 *Bicentennial History of Harrison, Maine, 1905-2005*, 2005; Owatonna Capital Campaign, 2000, Phoebe (Pemy) MacKenzie Smith Collection; Scott Coolidge, "Camp Owatonna Alumni Site," n.d., www.campowatonna.com.

294 Echo Newsletter, August 20, 1966; Author's interview with Jamie Bollinger.

295 Author's interview with Jamie Bollinger.

296 Email from Scott Moeller, November 8, 2020.

297 Author's interview with Jamie Bollinger.

298 Jim Cossey, "Race History," *Call of the Loon*, Fall 2017.

299 Author's interview with Jamie Bollinger; Author's interview with Seth Johnson.

300 Email from Jim Cossey, January 21, 2021; Bollinger, *100 Years at Camp Newfound, 1914-2013*; Cossey, "Race History."

301 Author's interview with Marcia Martin, May 28, 2021; Newfound/Owatonna Newsletter, Winter 2000.

302 Email from Duncan Wilder, June 6, 2020.

303 Great Race documents, Evan MacDonald Collection.

304 Christian Cole, 40th Annual Star Island Conference, Institute on Religion in an Age of Science.

305 Email from James S. Rosebush, January 17, 2021; "Paul Christian Cole."

306 Camp photo album, 1978, Phoebe (Pemy) MacKenzie Smith Collection.

307 Author's interview with Burt Cady.

308 "Camp Owatonna," *Christian Science Monitor*, May 14, 1982.

309 Email from Wells Sampson.

310 Author's interview with Jamie Bollinger.

311 Email from Wells Sampson.

312 "Camp Owatonna," *Christian Science Monitor*, March 9, 1981; "Camp Owatonna," May 14, 1982; Author's interview with Burt Cady.

313 Author's interview with Rich Coomber.

314 Author's interview with Rich Coomber.

315 Author's interview with Burt Cady.

316 "Daycroft School History," Daycroft School, n.d., https://www.daycroftschool.org/daycroft-school-history/; Author's interview with Erik Olsen.

317 Author's interview with Rich Coomber.

318 Principia College Catalog Supplement, 1981.

319 Author's interview with Dave Pelton, May 28, 2021.

320 Brad Jealous, "An Adventure I Will Not Forget," Owatonna/Newfound News, May 1997, Phoebe (Pemy) MacKenzie Smith Collection.

321 Author's interview with Dave Pelton. Trips to Popham seem to have ceased in the late 2000s.

322 Bollinger, *100 Years at Camp Newfound, 1914-2013*.

323 Bollinger.

324 Bollinger; Camps Newfound/Owatonna, Inc. v. Town of Harrison et al. (U.S. Supreme Court October 1996). Email from Lindsey Gorman, August 2021.

325 Email from Scott Moeller, February 2, 2021; *Bicentennial History of Harrison, Maine, 1905-2005*, 2005.

326 The hockey court is not seen in a 1986 slideshow but is seen in a 1992 slideshow, both created by Scott Coolidge; see https://vimeo.com/184883810 and https://vimeo.com/187483710. Interviewees recall the court existing in the late 1980s.

327 Author's interview with Marcia Martin.

328 Author's interview with Seth Johnson.

329 Author's interview with Marcia Martin; Newfound/Owatonna Newsletter, Winter 2000.

330 Owatonna Staff List, 1989, Evan MacDonald Collection.

331 Author's interview with Seth Johnson.

332 Author's interview with Weldon Rutledge.

333 Owatonna Capital Campaign; Coolidge, "Camp Owatonna Alumni Site."

334 *Bicentennial History of Harrison, Maine, 1905-2005.*

335 Author's interview with Seth Johnson.

336 Author's interview with Jamie Bollinger.

337 Author's interview with Jamie Bollinger; Owatonna Capital Campaign.

338 Camps Newfound/Owatonna Identity Statement, April 1990, Phoebe (Pemy) MacKenzie Smith Collection.

339 Author's interview with Seth Johnson.

340 Author's interview with David Taylor, February 20, 2021.

341 Owatonna Capital Campaign.

342 Newfound/Owatonna Newsletter, May 1996.

343 Jill Whitchurch, "Chief of Facilities Peter Whitchurch Retires," *Call of the Loon*, Fall 2014.

344 Whitchurch.

345 Author's interview with Forrest Bless, June 2, 2021; Author's interview with Reid Charlston, May 26, 2021.

346 Author's interview with Reid Charlston.

347 Author's interview with Forrest Bless.

348 Author's interview with Jamie Bollinger.

349 Author's interview with Jamie Bollinger.

350 Owatonna Newsletter, August 1999, Camp Owatonna Archive.

351 Owatonna Newsletter.

352 Robert Marquand, "High Court Frees Charities from Property-Tax Pinch," *Christian Science Monitor*, May 20, 1997.

353 Owatonna Capital Campaign.

354 Owatonna Capital Campaign; Author's interview with Jamie Bollinger.

355 Whitchurch, "Chief of Facilities Peter Whitchurch Retires"; Owatonna Newsletter, July 1999, Phoebe (Pemy) MacKenzie Smith Collection.

356 Author's interview with Jamie Bollinger.

357 Email from Duncan Wilder; Author's interview with Travis Brantingham, May 25, 2021.

358 Owatonna Newsletter - Second Session, Summer 2000, Camp Owatonna Archive.

359 Coolidge, "Camp Owatonna Alumni Site."

360 Owatonna Newsletter - First Session, Summer 2001, Camp Owatonna Archive.

361 Author's interview with Travis Brantingham.

362 Owatonna Newsletter - Second Session.

363 Bollinger, *100 Years at Camp Newfound, 1914-2013*; *Bicentennial History of Harrison, Maine, 1905-2005*, 2005; Newfound/Owatonna Newsletter, Winter 2000; Owatonna Newsletter - First Session.

364 Owatonna Newsletter - Second Session.

365 Newfound/Owatonna Newsletter, Winter 2000.

366 Author's interview with Jamie Bollinger.

367 "Adding Adventure to P.E.," *Principia Purpose*, Winter 2009.

368 Author's interview with Travis Brantingham.

369 Author's interview with Travis Brantingham.

370 Author's interview with Evan MacDonald, May 28, 2021.

371 Email from Duncan Wilder.

372 Email from Duncan Wilder.

373 Staff Goals and Expectations, Summer 2004, Evan MacDonald Collection; Author's interview with Mike Vernon, July 2021.

374 Author's interview with Travis Brantingham.

375 Author's interview with Evan MacDonald.

376 Whitchurch, "Chief of Facilities Peter Whitchurch Retires."

377 Author's interview with Travis Brantingham.

378 Email from Duncan Wilder.

379 Email from Brandon Frank, June 14, 2021.

380 "Men's Track and Field Roster," University of Texas at Austin, 2008, https://texassports.com/sports/mens-track-and-field/roster/erik-stanley/1122.

381 "Erik Stanley: Pro Trail Running Coach," RootsRated, May 9, 2016, https://rootsrated.com/stories/erik-stanley-pro-trail-running-coach.

382 Coolidge, "Camp Owatonna Alumni Site."

383 Bollinger, *100 Years at Camp Newfound, 1914-2013*.

384 Frank, "Putting on the 'New Man.'"

385 Author's interview with Forrest Bless.

386 Author's interview with Forrest Bless.

387 Author's interview with Forrest Bless.

388 Email from Duncan Wilder.

389 Author's interview with Evan MacDonald.

390 Author's interview with Dave Pelton.

391 Author's interview with Jamie Bollinger.

[392] Author's interview with Dave Pelton.

[393] Author's interview with Dave Pelton.

[394] Author's interview with Dave Pelton; Author's interview with Jamie Bollinger.

[395] Author's interview with Jamie Bollinger.

[396] Author's interview with Dave Pelton.

[397] Whitchurch, "Chief of Facilities Peter Whitchurch Retires."

[398] Author's interview with Dave Pelton.

[399] Author's interview with Reid Charlston.

[400] Author's interview with Reid Charlston.

[401] Author's interview with Reid Charlston.

INDEX

Anderson, Ty, 58, 59, 66, 70, 74, 81, 88, 89, 92, 93, 160, 170, 181

Awards
  "R" Camper (Ropioa), 27, 69
  Arrowheads, 153
  Black Feather, 24, 69, 77, 91, 102, 109, 159, 184
  Triple Crown Winner, 109, 110, 159, 160, 170, 200
  White Feather, 69, 70, 77, 91

Baker, Ervin, 77, 78, 127, 141, 142

Baker, Pearl, 77, 92, 141, 142

Batty, Terry, 90, 202

Beyer, Eric, 99, 100, 202

Beyer, Fred, 93, 98, 99, 181

Bless, Forrest, 145, 146, 168, 169, 170, 171, 181, 202

Bliss, Jr., Donald T., 66, 89

Bole, Eric, 68

Bollinger, Jamie, 99, 100, 109, 110, 118, 119, 120, 126, 131, 139, 142, 146, 147, 148, 149, 153, 154, 155, 157, 171, 172, 173, 181, 201, 202

Bower, Bonnie, 103, 106, 107, 114, 149

Bower, John, 103, 106, 107, 108, 110, 112, 113, 114, 117, 130, 139, 147, 169, 175, 181

Brantingham, Travis, 152, 153, 154, 155, 156, 157, 158, 159, 160, 169, 181, 202

Brewster, Buz, 77, 80, 102

Cady, Burt, 124, 125, 126, 128, 181, 202

Camps
  Leelanau, 49, 50, 54, 56, 58, 60, 68, 78, 133, 140, 155, 156, 157, 159, 169
  Long Lake Lodge, 40, 196
  O-AT-KA, 39, 72, 140, 156

Passaconaway, 40, 41, 48, 58, 89
Ranger Lodge, 80
Sunapee, 121
Takajo, 39
Tawasi, 40, 42
Wigwam, 39, 56, 140, 156, 171
Wingo, 80
Winona, 39, 140, 156
Wyonee, 40
Zakelo, 80, 196

Chaplin, Joseph S., 4, 5, 8, 9, 41, 78

Charlston, Reid, 145, 146, 169, 175, 176, 177, 181, 202

Cherry Island, 5, 78, 92, 102, 122, 148, 196

Christian Science, 3, 22, 36, 37, 40, 41, 49, 67, 70, 72, 73, 74, 92, 99, 108, 118, 125, 129, 142, 143, 154, 155, 156, 170, 171, 175, 176
  Mary Baker Eddy, 33, 74, 119, 154

Clark, Bob, 129, 130, 155, 181

Cobb, Dorothy Horton, 47, 48, 49, 50, 92

Cole, Chris, 116, 117, 118, 119, 120, 121, 122, 125, 133, 181

Connor, Frank Hayden, 2, 3, 10, 37, 47, 48, 49, 50, 51, 72, 76, 92, 100, 103, 201

Connor, Phoebe Ann, 47, 48, 49, 134

Connor, Phoebe Fischer, 48

Coomber, Rich, 109, 120, 121, 126, 127, 129, 201, 202

Cooper, John McGill, 13, 48, 92

Crandell, Gary, 108, 129, 130, 131, 132, 181, 202

Daycroft School, 99, 101, 129, 133

DeMascola, Benjamin, 42, 47, 48, 92

Edwards, Phil, 2, 56, 66, 67, 68, 69, 71, 72, 73, 74, 75, 76, 77, 78, 80, 81, 89, 90, 92, 100, 102, 109, 110, 125, 146, 181

Frank, Brandon, 160, 162, 169, 170, 181, 202

Harter, Nolen, 90, 100, 102, 202

Heim, Hal, 20, 21, 23, 25, 34, 36

Herberich, Jim, 117, 118

Hilton, Tom, 49, 50, 51, 54, 55, 56, 58, 59, 60, 67, 68, 92, 181

Horton, Elizabeth, 1, 5

Johnson, Glenn, 109, 111, 139, 200, 201

Johnson, Seth "Chic", 108, 110, 111, 119, 120, 121, 133, 138, 139, 142, 143, 160, 181, 202

Jones, Boyd N., 48

LaMarsh, John, 37, 39, 40, 41, 42, 50

Lowe, Donald S., 13, 32, 33, 34, 181

MacDonald, Evan, 156, 158, 171, 201, 202

MacRae, Gordon, 79

Martin, Peter, 111, 121, 132, 133, 134, 139, 141, 153, 155, 173, 181

Moeller, Scott, 92, 109, 120, 202

Newfound, Camp, 1, 3, 4, 5, 22, 24, 25, 34, 35, 39, 40, 41, 47, 48, 49, 55, 72, 90, 91, 92, 100, 107, 108, 109, 110, 112, 113, 114, 120, 126, 130, 131, 132, 139, 145, 148, 158, 161, 173, 174, 177

Ogallala Golds, 103, 117, 118, 146, 160, 192
   Native American origins, 103

Owatonna
   4 on the Fourth, 120, 121, 160
   Council Fire, 12, 23, 40, 56, 70, 71, 73, 76, 91, 101, 109, 126, 134
   Flag Trip, 140, 141, 157
   Gitchi-Gumi, 22, 147, 157
   Hill Run, 75, 80, 92, 110, 147, 148
   Mountain Man Challenge, 157, 158, 161
   The Great Race, 121
   Track Meet, 147, 157
   Water Carnival, 91, 148
   Woodsman, 157

Pelton, Dave, 130, 169, 171, 172, 173, 174, 181, 202

Penobscot Blues, 56, 68, 76, 109, 110, 188
   Native American origins, 25, 26, 57

Pequawket Greens, 56, 57, 69, 76, 80, 132, 135, 159, 160, 170, 186
   Native American origins, 57

Principia
   College, 67, 89, 93, 102, 114, 118, 130, 139, 143, 144, 146, 160, 169, 171, 175
   Lower School, 155
   Upper School, 68, 89, 129, 130, 133

Romero, Al, 13, 37, 47, 48, 79

Rupp, Bill, 36, 37, 202

Sampson, Wells, 117, 118, 125, 130, 133, 202

Schlueter, Jack, 120, 147

Schneider, Chris "Skip", 147

Scholet, Art, 76

Schulze, Bruce, 117, 181

Shawsheen Reds, 56, 69, 75, 76, 80, 102, 110, 126, 146, 157, 158, 190
   Native American origins, 56

Singer, Ray "Doc", 66, 75, 78, 92

Snyder, Zack, 126

Stackhouse, Peter, 81

Stanley, George A., 1, 2, 3, 9, 10, 11, 12, 24, 26, 27, 34, 36, 37, 38, 47, 49, 181

Stanley, Gertrude, 1, 2, 3, 4, 5, 10, 27, 36, 37, 38, 41, 48

Stevens, William, 2, 25

Swanson, Terry, 68, 69

Taylor, David, 143, 144, 146, 181, 202

Trilsch, Robert, 22, 25, 48

Ullom, Verne, 98, 99, 102, 103, 181

Wattawasso, Princess, 25, 26

Whitchurch, Peter, 144, 145, 155, 158, 170, 174, 175

Youngblood, David, 41, 58, 59, 68, 69, 70, 71, 202

About the Author

J. R. Suber was a camper and counselor at Camp Owatonna during the 2000s. He was on the Golds team, but he unfortunately missed each summer they won 1st place—perhaps there is a correlation. He was a C.I.T. in 2005 and a J.C. in 2006. As a counselor, he spent much of his time at the Owatonna Beach. Among his favorite memories is waking up early to play rugby with his fellow counselors on the field across Route 35. He is most proud of his tie for Most Personals in 2003.

Made in the USA
Coppell, TX
22 August 2021